How We Vote

How We Vote

The Factors That Influence Voters

Surjit S. Bhalla

with

Abhinav Motheram

🌀 juggernaut

JUGGERNAUT BOOKS
C-I-128, First Floor, Sangam Vihar, Near Holi Chowk,
New Delhi 110080, India

First published by Juggernaut Books 2024

10 9 8 7 6 5 4 3 2 1

P-ISBN: 9789353458430
E-ISBN: 9789353453671

Typeset in Adobe Caslon Pro by R. Ajith Kumar, Noida

Printed at Nutech Print Services - India

For my most discerning critic,
Ravinder – love and jugalbandi

Contents

Contents

1

Democracy and Choice

Elections are both a serious and naughty business. First, the serious part. It is about the future of people, their lives and *good* roads to their governance. That was always the case; only now, social media has compounded the problem to such an extent that some would say it is beyond repair. Be it the war in Ukraine or the atrocities in Israel–Palestine (is Israel the erstwhile Palestine or vice versa?) or the ongoing elections in many places around the world, truth is in jeopardy, and there is no one to ease the pain by pronouncing the 'truth'.

It is increasingly difficult to define, let alone identify, a truth. There is artificial intelligence, fake news and even worse, fake expert commentary. There is a lot of information. How does one sift through the misinformation or the ideologically laced commentary to identify the disinformation?!

All of this affects the choices of a billion people in 2024.

There is a lot to debate, to fight for and to choose. For the people of India, the choice is, as in all elections, the same. Do you want the incumbent to continue, or do you want a change of guard?

This book is about this very important choice – what determines it, what has determined it in the past and, tentatively, what is the 2024 choice likely to be? We will pay a lot of attention to the first two questions and explore them in detail; pointers to Choice 2024 may be implicit in our discussion and analysis. This is not a suspense novel – it is, rather, a reading, and perhaps an interpretation, of the political and economic tea leaves.

Let's lay down some basic ground rules of discussion and discourse. No analysis or discussion of what the writers *hope* will happen will occur in this book. In the last chapter, we discuss the hopes and desires for the future of Bharat/ India. We recognize that preferences, especially political preferences, are sometimes moral, sometimes pragmatic and often instinctive and straight from the gut. But that does not mean the individuals making the choices have not thought through the arguments.

Outlooks differ in the arguments, as does the reasoning. For some, the 'absolute' argument is paramount, i.e. X has done something, but she should not have done it. And hence, she will not get my vote.

But there are hardly any absolutes – not in life and especially not in politics. The art of the possible is what politics is about, and the possible is sometimes mighty difficult. Take, for instance, the fact that the farm bill was not passed even though one would have thought it was well within the realm of the possible.

Protests erupted from within the Opposition Congress party and spread to Greta Thunberg and Rihanna over well-organized networks. Yet, the Punjab Congress government itself had proposed the same or similar changes via a report written by the former deputy of the Planning Commission and a leading economic reformer, Montek Singh Ahluwalia. Similar reforms were included in Congress's 2019 election manifesto. Yet, the 'liberals' opposed the farm laws, en masse. A one-hour video interview I gave from my office as executive director at the International Monetary Fund (IMF) analysing the farm agitation was not telecast, while others supporting the protests were.

Besides the warning of absolute versus relative arguments, the reader should heed an additional warning about narratives and reality. Today, the line between narratives and perceived reality is disturbingly thin – we live in a polarized world, and want to believe what we want to believe. Polarization is a global phenomenon. Opinions, and people, have become hard-wired. Aided and abetted by tendentious facts, misinformation and disinformation.

What is today called a 'narrative' – earlier used to be called 'spin'. Nobel Prize winner Robert Shiller discusses the increasingly dominant role of narratives in his outstanding book *Narrative Economics: How Stories Go Viral and Drive*

Major Economic Events. This comprehensive book is about all forms of narratives, stories that go viral, stories that are an actual reflection of reality and stories that aren't quite so. The last chapter, entitled 'Future Narratives, Future Research', is from where we borrow our version of narrative. In this chapter Shiller states, 'A problem in using narratives to forecast economic variables is that human judgement and *discourse about narratives tend to be politicized and emotion-ridden*' [emphasis added]. Shiller's book is a must read for all interested in 'identifying the truth' and knowing how a rational mind often falls for an irrational story, spin or narrative. One description of a 'future' narrative? A collection of 'facts' persuasively argued to serve an ideological agenda.

Our contribution to the debate on facts, if any, is to dispassionately provide the data, the arguments, so that the reader can form her own conclusions. We will attempt to provide all sides of the evidence so the reader can intelligently make inferences about Choice 2024.

What determines our vote? This depends on whether we are talking about today, yesterday or tomorrow. Not to be cute but one of the big stories about this election is that India is in transition from a lower-middle-income to a middle-income economy today and a developed economy tomorrow.

I can see the sceptics guffawing. Yes, we have seen this movie before, in India Shining 2004. Indeed, there is a whole chapter devoted to what happened in 2004, and why we think 2004 was likely the beginning of the journey of India Shining rather than its completion.

Today, there is considerable evidence to buttress the belief that India is well on the road to shining, which we will provide. There are those who think or hope, some even loudly, that the Opposition I.N.D.I.A. alliance can pull off a 2004. They may choose to ignore the 'India Shining' data because that evidence does not mesh with their thoughts. But they may also be living in Dreamland or a parallel universe.

That's the tomorrow. Today is different. It is election year, and hence descriptions of reality come with a deep discount. Even in normal times, economic data is hotly contested and election years are not 'normal' in India. Examples of opinions masquerading as truths abound, which are discussed in detail.

Let us look at data on the labour market, i.e. unemployment and labour force participation. Candidate Bill Clinton aptly described his 1992 campaign as one revolving around the economy – *It's the economy, stupid* is now a household phrase the world over. India is four times more populous and many, many times more varied than the US. Not unexpectedly, there is so much variation in the data that almost anyone can come out with an observation or a description that 'fits' the chosen narrative.

This is the era of narratives, and given it is an election year in India, the narratives are having their day in the limelight. For example, observe the take on female labour force participation rate (FLFPR) in India, as presented by a private data provider, Centre for Monitoring Indian Economy (CMIE).

Claudia Goldin deservedly got a long-overdue Nobel Prize for her work on the levels and changes in the female workforce in the US. Even before the prize, FLFPR in India, according to CMIE, was a big story. Why? Because according to CMIE, India's FLFPR in 2023, at 9%, was not just the lowest in the world but lower than war-torn countries like Yemen and Iraq – hence indicative of all not being well with the economy. The latest official estimate of FLFPR is close to 40%, i.e. more than four times higher. Yet, the appeal of the narrative in election year India is so strong that there are hardly any (none!?) calling out the CMIE bluff. (This is discussed in great detail in the chapter on gender equity, Chapter 9.)

If it is the economy that matters most (it does matter a lot) and if the Indian economy is looking good (GDP data, IMF and the World Bank are all in agreement), then it is logical that the narrative of the Opposition is going to be that the economy is not doing well, and its calling card will be WYSINWYG – what you see is *not* what you get. This counter-narrative has had, and is having, predictable second-round effects. Action is being delayed on much-needed reforms, e.g., farm laws. Further, the action and thinking on challenges to future sustained growth – e.g., policies needed to get India to a developed country status by 2047 – are being delayed.

As the chapters in this book reveal, India is in a sweet spot of growth. Actually, it may be a long-term sweet spot. But given our nature and politics, we don't necessarily recognize or appreciate the structural transformation that has already occurred and that is currently taking place.

Instead of discussing future challenges that face India as a nation – delimitation, the substitution of reservation for merit, providing good quality education from the primary level upwards – politicians are indulging in *revdis* (unwarranted freebies to portions of the electorate with the single objective of garnering votes for an upcoming election). This is different from vote-bank politics in which you favour one ethnic or religious or caste group with the single objective of co-opting them so that you can safely take them for granted.

I have long been a believer in the dictum that economics determines elections and investment in both physical and human capital determines growth and increase in welfare. However, arguments and dissent abound. Instead of agreement on the fundamentals and what can be done to maximize achievement, 'we' are preoccupied with false narratives. For example, you will hear that there is not enough investment for our growth, not enough taxes for finance and redistribution, that we have a K-shaped recovery merely providing jobs to the rich (meaning the rich are getting richer and the poor poorer) and there are no jobs for women!

Discourse and evidence pointers

This book will provide three guideposts (and, in equal measure, goalposts) for discussion. First, it is important that one changes one's mind (narrative?) when confronted with strong evidence that challenges one's prior view or recommendations. John Maynard Keynes, an original liberal, said it best when he stated, 'When facts change, I change my mind. What do you do, Madam?'

The second pointer comes from the movie *Jerry Maguire*, where a football player keeps asking his agent for evidence about his job prospects, particularly his salary prospects. He keeps repeating 'Show me the money', which can be paraphrased for this book to 'Show me the evidence'.

The third benchmark of evidence in a narrative world is the difficulty in identifying the truth, the reality, the facts. What passes for evidence today is the Rashomon Effect (an expression derived from the movie *Rashomon*, which shows the same incident from the perspective of multiple people). Each of us have our own facts and, therefore, our own interpretation of the truth. In all of this noise, amplified many times by social media, how is one to act on the unknown truth? Remember, every mistruth is likely to have an element of truth embedded in it. Which is why identifying the 'most truthful' among all the competing Rashomon truths is so difficult.

But we must attempt to do so. Towards this end, this book reports a lot of data, perhaps too much. But one cannot challenge entrenched beliefs and ideological passion with traditional tools. Instead, we must rely on data.

And before reporting on the topics considered, let me get another shrug of the shoulder out of the way. Individuals, especially those whose opinion or 'fact' I disagree with, find it easy to dismiss the idea with the line 'Surjit is just being contrarian'. That is not an incorrect statement. I am being contrarian. There is no point in regurgitating agreements, especially on important debates. Hence, it is indeed the case that there are many agreements among the disagreements. The former are not reported in the interest of discourse and space!

Chapter 2 is the start of our journey with a discussion about the political and economic reality of India – from the first election year 1952 to 2024. We discuss elections and the major determinants of their outcomes. One interesting economic fact revealed by the data is that a much talked about determinant (inflation mistakenly labelled 'price rise') has had precious little to do with the contours of any national election!

Chapter 3 is titled 'The Challenge of the Nehru Record'. Nehru won three consecutive elections, a rare event in politics worldwide. There is a likelihood that Mr Modi will join this exclusive club this year. Chapters 4 and 5 discuss the state of democracy in the world – is the world really becoming less democratic, and how accurate are international rankings of Indian democracy?

Chapter 5 is about the micro-elements of democracy in India – the 'treatment' and 'outcomes' of minorities, the poor and the women. This directly leads us to an extended discussion (Chapter 6) of claims made by Sabyasachi Das (2023) (at the time of the release of his working paper, he was an assistant professor at the Ashoka University), that in all the Indian elections to date, the 2019 election in which the Bharatiya Janata Party (BJP) won 303 seats is the only one with 'strong' evidence of vote manipulation by the ruling party (the BJP).

Chapters 7 through 11 are devoted to economic data and narratives. Chapter 7 looks at 'accusations' about GDP growth in India being overstated – only during the present Modi regime of the last ten years and never before! (Note the coincidental similarity with Das's contention of electoral overstatement by the BJP in 2019 and never before.) Chapter 7 also examines the likelihood of other vote-getting achievements being the present high level of GDP growth, comparisons with the period of high growth during the 2004–13 United Progressive Alliance (UPA) regime, as well as 'promises' of India being a $5 trillion economy and the expectation of India being a developed economy by 2047. The Opposition, at least as gleaned through some writings on the subject, believes that these promises are less than accurate and part of the 'feel-good' narrative of the Modi government.

Chapter 8 looks at the super important issue of employment and unemployment. Even before the 2019 election, there was considerable discussion of Modi's so-called 'promise' of 10 million jobs a year. This was much exaggerated, according to the doubters. It turns out that the economy did much better than 10 million jobs a year between 2014 and 2023.

Chapter 9 deals with several issues related to gender equity in India. The progress on education, labour force participation, unemployment and jobs, and male–female wage gaps are all examined in some detail.

Chapter 10 deals with yet another contentious political and economic issue – how much has *Garibi* (poverty) been *Hataoed* (eradicated) in India – both under Modi and the earlier governments (especially 2004–13).

Chapter 11, 'Redistribution with Growth', is on a subject we believe history will define as years – the last ten years – where, almost uniquely among developing (and developed) nations, a considerable amount of redistribution was achieved in India along with healthy economic growth.

Chapter 12 discusses in elaborate detail the expected contours of voting in 2024 as we see them in February 2024. How effective will the I.N.D.I.A. alliance be? Has the alliance followed known unknowns about what it takes to dislodge a popular leader? Has the Congress been excessively feudal about its expected alliance with other members of I.N.D.I.A.? And we present a lot of data to substantiate our expectations about Choice 2024.

Our concluding chapter, Chapter 13, is about the challenges ahead. Some challenges considered: delimitation and the north–south divide; reform of agriculture and the introduction of long-overdue farm laws; reform of direct taxes (lower average income tax rate); reform of GST (make it more progressive and lower effective GST rate); and last, and probably the most needed reform – overhaul reform and modernization of our statistical system. Throughout this book, I talk about how both statistical delivery (by the government) and statistical reception (by civil society) are grossly inadequate for a modern nation, let alone a country aspiring to be a developed economy, and within touching distance of becoming the third largest economy in the world.

2

What Determines Our Vote?
Caste, Religion, Economy?

How do we vote?

What a question – 'Of course it is caste or religion, or both' is the knee-jerk response.

Note that these two concerns at present are determining what the Opposition seems to be offering and what the Opposition thinks Modi's BJP is offering. Bihar, under the guidance and encouragement of Nitish Kumar, conducted the first state caste census in India. There have been two national-level caste censuses in India. The first in 1931 and the second Socio-Economic Caste Census (SECC) in 2011. SECC census data has never been released, though brief summary data are available. The non-release of the 2011 data should have been a signal to Nitish Kumar, chief minister of Bihar and one who authorized the state survey. This was (to be) Nitish's calling card for a national unity campaign, in comparison and in contrast to the Bharat Jodo Yatra of Rahul Gandhi's Congress.

It almost worked. Nitish Kumar was believed to be the great unifier of the Opposition. Remember, he broke off with Modi and the National Democratic Alliance (NDA) before election 2014. Nitish's gambit failed – he is now back with the BJP and Modi. Nitish says he left the Opposition alliance because the Congress did not offer him respect or leadership.

We believe the caste census was more of a damp squib, an idea out of tune with reality and aspirations. There are very good reasons why a caste census has not been held since 1931. Modi's consistent appeal is to a modern India, an aspiring India. An India that wants to benefit the poor via redistribution on the basis of income, not on the basis of birth records. That is the reality that the usually savvy Nitish missed.

Regarding religion, the Ram Janmabhoomi temple has been built, something that has been deeply desired by Hindus. It is a mistake to interpret this action as anti-secular, which many so-called 'secular' Hindus are arrogantly articulating.

The very definition of secularism is an environment where all individuals, not just minority individuals, can practise their religion without any pangs of guilt.

That is where the anti-religion Nehru went wrong. The religious Hindu will ask: Why is it that Muslims, Sikhs and Christians (not to mention Jews and Buddhists and Jains and atheists) can freely and proudly practice their religion, and the 80% majority Hindu cannot? *Yeh kahan ka nyay hai?* (Wherefrom this concept of justice?) The Ram Mandir appeals to this constituency and the BJP bet is that it outnumbers the secularist.

To get back to what matters when we vote. I have no doubt that Modi and the BJP will get credit for giving birth to a newer, 'truer' secularism from many voters. The Opposition is likely to offer the building of the Ram Mandir complex as an excuse as to why they lost the 2024 election if indeed the BJP comes back to power.

But as the contents in this book make a great effort to document, the real reason that Indians are likely to vote in Modi for the third time is because they believe his government has resurrected hope, aspirations and welfare across broad masses of people, especially the 'poor'. The reason I have put poor in quote marks is because the definition of poor in India today is no longer absolute but *relative* to per capita income. Hence, it can involve a larger fraction of people than what an absolute level of poverty would dictate. Note that the 2013 Food Security Act envisioned food subsidies to the bottom two-thirds of the population believed to be poor – 50% of urban India and 75% of rural. One of the choices facing the new government in 2024 is whether India needs a poverty definition consistent with the soon-to-be-reality of a $5 trillion economy.

Choice 2024 – what matters

There are several determinants of voting choices – religion, caste, economy – but the record yields the intuitive result – it is the economy, stupid.

In my book *Citizen Raj* (March 2019), I analysed Indian

elections between 1952 and 2014 and reached the same conclusion – economic performance mattered the most. The last paragraph of my 2002 book *Imagine There's No Country* (p. 206) started with the question, 'Can growth alone be sufficient for poverty reduction?' And ended with 'the conclusion differs from the conventional wisdom that "attacking poverty requires actions beyond the economic domain". Such actions are not needed. Growth is sufficient, period.'

Not everyone agreed with me. And in his recent book, India's ace psephologist Pradip Gupta, who has made many correct forecasts, boldly asks the question, 'Why does GDP growth have almost no impact on election outcomes?' Those are fighting words, especially for someone whose research has consistently shown the opposite! (See *Citizen Raj* for a sampling.)

Our first attempt in this chapter is to review India's electoral and economic history over the last 75 years and see whether growth affects electoral outcomes. We paint election years with a very broad brush. Which means we are not trying to be definitive but rather informative. The first electoral hypothesis we will examine is the effectiveness of *per capita* (pc) growth in real GDP as a predictor of elections. It is admittedly a crude index, but as you will see, it is revealing.

A broad economic sweep of history

India gained independence in 1947, became a republic in 1950 and in 1952 had its first parliamentary election. Our first prime minister was Jawaharlal Nehru, and he won three consecutive elections, a record that still stands today even if the tea leaves suggest that the record will be equalled in 2024. But more on that in the rest of the chapters.

Table 2.1 presents some basic statistics on the Indian economy, organized according to Lok Sabha elections since 1952 and soon-to-be-held 2024 election.

For each election period, three important indicators are presented – growth in population, price level (inflation) and welfare (given by pc GDP growth). If the first three elections are ignored, then a simple eyeballing of the data suggests that a 3–3.5% or an average of 3.25% in per capita growth was a reasonable proxy for welfare improvement in the first four decades post-Independence.

Table 2.1: A Simple Model of Per Capita Growth and Election Victory (%)

| | | Growth in | | | | Election Model | |
Election Year	Period	Popula-tion	Prices	pc GDP	Incum-bent	Predicted Winner	Right (✓) Wrong (✗)
1957	1952–56	1.7	0.2	1.8	INC		
1962	1957–61	1.9	2.6	-0.7	INC	–	–
1967	1962–66	2.1	7.7	0.8	INC	TF	✗
1971	1967–70	2.1	5.0	3.4	INC	INC	✓
1977	1971–76	2.3	8.0	0.3	INC	TF	✓

Election Year	Period	Growth in			Incum-bent	Election Model	
		Popula-tion	Prices	pc GDP		Predicted Winner	Right (✓) Wrong (✗)
1980	1977–79	2.3	5.5	0	TF	INC	✓
1984	1980–83	2.3	10.5	3.4	INC	INC	✓
1989	1984–88	2.2	7.3	3.1	INC	TF	✓
1991	1989–90	2.1	7.5	3.5	TF	INC	✗
1996	1991–95	2.0	9.7	3.0	INC	TF	✓
1998	1996–97	1.9	7.8	3.7	TF	BJP	✓
1999	1998	1.8	12.3	4.2	BJP	BJP	✓
2004	1999–2003	1.7	4.2	3.9	BJP	BJP	✗
2009	2004–08	1.5	5.9	6.1	INC	INC	✓
2014	2009–13	1.3	9.8	5.9	INC	INC	✗
2019	2014–18	1.1	4.3	6.0	BJP	BJP	✓
2024	2019–23	0.9	5.3	3 or >5	BJP	BJP	✓

Source: Election Commission of India, CEIC; author's calculations

Notes: (1) The results from 'growth only' mode suggest a shorthand rule for the re-election - per capita (pc) GDP growth during the tenure is above 3.25%.

(2) For example, between 1962 and 1966 the Congress ruled and delivered an average pc growth of 0.8%, below the 3.2%.

(3) The BJP is forecast to win the 2024 election because average GDP growth in the non-Covid years 2021–22 to 2023–24 will be well above 7%!

Until the 1996 elections, population growth averaged more than 2% per year, so a 3.25% pc growth really meant a 5% plus GDP growth. The growth to election model is a very simple one – did per capita GDP growth exceed 3.25% during the election period immediately preceding the election? The assumption is that voters vote the pocketbook, not their caste or religion or their 'ideology'. A higher than

3.25% per annum growth would nudge the voter to vote for the incumbent; a lower than 3.25%, would nudge the voter to oust the incumbent. For example, in 1967 the Congress (helmed by Indira Gandhi) was the incumbent, the preceding five years of Congress rule had yielded a growth rate of only 0.8% per annum, so Congress should have lost. It won, yielding a failure for our first prediction!

The table lists only three victors – the Congress, BJP, and a generic non-BJP–non-Congress alliance which we term a Third Front. The Congress lost power in 1977, 1989 and 1996. Three different Opposition alliances gained power in these years – and in all three, the victor is labelled as TF (Third Front). Note also that the economic situation in India remained broadly the same between 1947 and 1991, with some minimalist economic reforms being introduced by Prime Minister Rajiv Gandhi during his tenure, 1984 to 1989.

The Election Model column shows how accurate the model is with a '✓' denoting a correct decision and '✗' (failure) otherwise. After 1967, the model also gets the 1991 election wrong, but the model did correctly predict Rajiv Gandhi's loss in 1989. Per capita growth during the Rajiv Gandhi years was a low 3.1%, and V.P. Singh, finance minister under Rajiv Gandhi, won the election on the grounds of high intensity corruption. The coalition era was born, and the economy continued to deteriorate. Growth during the period 1989–90 was just above the 3.25%

threshold, so the Third Front led by Chandra Shekhar should have won in 1991. But India was plunged into a debt crisis and had to seek an emergency IMF loan of $2.2 billion, something the simple growth to election model cannot incorporate.

Rajiv Gandhi was assassinated in May 1991, and a new Congress led coalition minority government was formed under Narasimha Rao; the party won only 244 seats out of a total strength of 543. The coalition era continued. Major economic reforms were introduced, and India grew at a respectable 7% plus per annum for three successive years. Despite this record achievement, the Congress lost the 1996 election, winning only 140 seats. The 1991 to 1995 growth average was only 3%, and hence the Congress loss in 1996 was well 'predicted'. Despite the correct prediction, it is ambiguous, and debatable, as to why the Congress lost by such a big margin in 1996.

Despite the 1996 loss, the BIG contribution of Narasimha Rao was that economic reforms became popular, and politicians felt that reforms were necessary for political success. The reform bug had caught the imagination of the Indian politician – all governments contributed to reforms, some more than others. Perhaps the Congress suffered from the pioneer first-mover disadvantage.

The next model prediction error is the 2004 election. Per capita GDP growth averaged 3.9% between 1999 and 2003, yet the BJP lost the election. This 'error in prediction' is discussed in detail later. The next, and last error to date, is the 2014 election. However, it is important to remember that despite average to good growth, the period was a turbulent one in terms of inflation, exchange rate depreciation and corruption (hence, per capita growth is not a *sufficient* predictor!). Also remember that despite 'high growth' no one can recall a single major economic reform during 2004–13, and especially 2009-13, to account for a respectable 6% average per capita growth during this period.

Prediction errors are part and parcel of forecasts. The 2024 election is another challenge for the model. The preceding five years per capita GDP growth is below the 3.25% cut-off, hence Modi should lose. But 2019–23 also includes the worst economic and human crisis (Covid) to befall the world since World War II. If we exclude the Covid year 2020–21 (which one should!), per capita growth has averaged 5.7%; if both 2020–21 and recovery year 2021–22 are excluded, then the average of 5.1% is still well above the win requirement of 3.25%. Hence, Covid adjusted, Modi should win the 2024 election. If the BJP does win the 2024 election, the 'only growth' model would have managed to get 10 out of 14 right. Not bad for just growth determining election outcomes.

Inflation as a non-predictor of elections

It used to be inflation and employment, but now worldwide, inflation is in retreat. There is a 20-plus-year history to this retreat, and it was only interrupted during the Covid crisis of 2020–22, and the policy response of governments was to pump their way out of a medical crisis by invoking a high level of unguarded deficit spending. The Western nations were the major culprits in pump-priming, though it has to be admitted that the road to inflation recovery was halted, and reversed, by the Russia–Ukraine war. Further, the post-Covid inflation increase could have happened anyway, because of a severe mismatch in the recovery (increase in demand) and an increase in supply bottlenecks.

Every election opinion poll in India shows that inflation matters for the voter. Time after time this is proven wrong, but pollsters (and Opposition politicians) love to get percentages stating that the electorate is concerned about 'price rise'. A more nonsensical polling question was never asked, and in the opinion polls I was involved in (1980s and 1990s), I avoided asking a question relating to 'price rise'. Unfortunately, the rich will always be with us, and with upgraded poverty lines, so will the poor. So will 'price rise'.

The inflation question should instead be 'Does it matter to you that inflation has accelerated/decelerated during the last X years?' But as you will no doubt agree, this question does not pass the KISS (Keep It Simple, Stupid) test for an opinion poll. Hence, my suggestion and conclusion is to avoid any questions relating to inflation.

For whatever it is worth, the Vajpayee-led BJP government had the lowest inflation record in India post 1960, and yet lost the 2004 election. Inflation between 1992 and 1997 averaged 8.6%. I am omitting the high inflation crisis year 1991–92 when inflation (unless otherwise specified, all inflation discussion is in terms of the Consumer Price Index) was a high 9.1%. During 1999–2003, inflation averaged 4.2%, the lowest India has ever experienced over an election period. Vajpayee also brought in several reforms, notably the lowering of high real deposit rates for small savings for example, as well as investment in infrastructure. In our opinion, he has not quite got the credit for putting growth and infrastructure investment on the map.

Reforms have a political cost and Vajpayee lost the 2004 election by a large margin. We explore the reasons behind this loss in Chapter 12. The prime beneficiary of BJP–Vajpayee reforms was not the BJP, but the Congress. GDP per capita growth averaged 6% from 2004 to 2013. Note that in Modi's first term, per capita growth also averaged 6%, making it 15 years in a row of 6% growth. The per capita growth equivalence puts into perspective the oft-repeated claim that GDP growth was faster under the UPA; this may be only because the UPA did not face a worldwide 'war' shock of Covid.[1]

3

The Challenge of the Nehru Record

At this moment, while the manuscript of *How We Vote* is nearing completion, the sole competitor to the BJP at the national level is the I.N.D.I.A. alliance. Most predictions from analysts and forecasts are that PM Modi will lead the BJP to a third successive victory.

There is a healthy debate on whether the BJP, on its own, will gain more than the 303 seats they won in 2019. In 2014, the BJP also won 9 seats more than the 273 seats required for a simple majority. If the widely forecast event happens, Modi would have won three consecutive national elections – and equalled Nehru's record.[1]

Only three PMs have won two consecutive elections in India since Nehru–Indira Gandhi in 1967 and 1971, Manmohan Singh (as head of two coalition governments in 2004 and 2009) and Narendra Modi in 2014 and 2019. The 2004 election was fought under the technical leadership of Ms Sonia Gandhi who then relinquished the prime ministership to Dr Manmohan Singh. As it happened, Manmohan Singh as the PM achieved the highest number of seats for the Congress since the 1991 election. The

Congress obtained 206 seats in 2009, strikingly close to Narasimha Rao's victory of 232 seats in 1991, and a large increase from the 145 seats won by Sonia Gandhi's Congress in 2004.

Winning three consecutive elections is a big deal in any democratic country, at any time. It is highly unusual. Let us look at the international record for parliamentary majority wins. Margaret Thatcher won three consecutive elections (1979, 1983 and 1987). George Washington won the first two elections unopposed, and then retired. Nelson Mandela did not seek re-election in 1999. In any case, the South African constitution (like the US) only allows two terms for any candidate. Franklin Roosevelt won four terms (1932, 1936, 1940 and 1944). The US law was then changed to not allow any person to serve more than two terms.

Table 3.1 documents the leading winners of consecutive terms in Indian state elections. Jyoti Basu, the Communist Party of India (Marxist) [CPM] leader of West Bengal, reigned supreme for 23 years. He won his first election in 1977 and his last in 1996. Naveen Patnaik's tenure (in days) has now exceeded that of Basu, and if he wins in 2024, he will exceed Basu's (and his own) record of five consecutive state wins. As the list shows, many chief ministers have won two consecutive terms; but the atmosphere is more rarefied for more than two consecutive wins.

It can be argued that consecutive wins in state elections are 'less difficult' than national victories. That is probably true. But Modi's record in state elections is also exceptional. He won in 2002, 2007 and 2012, and won with handsome victory margins – an average of 48.9% of the vote and 66% of the seats.

Neither Jyoti Basu nor Naveen Patnaik are close to this record. Basu's average vote and seat share in five elections was 37.6 and 60.2%, respectively. Patnaik's average record is almost identical to Basu: 36.7% average vote share and 62.7% average seat share. Tarun Gogoi of Congress won four terms with an average vote share of 35.5%, and average seat share of 45.8%. Only in the Northeast is Modi's vote and seat record challenged, most prominently by Pawan Kumar Chamling of Sikkim – five elections, average vote share of 57.3%, average seat share of 80%.

Table 3.1: Modi's Dominance as Chief Minister

Year	Vote Share (%)	Total	Contested	Won	Win Rate (%)
Narendra Modi – BJP, Gujarat					
2002	49.9	182	182	127	69.8
2007	48.9	182	182	116	63.7
2012	47.9	182	182	115	63.2
Jyoti Basu – CPM, West Bengal					
1977	35.5	294	224	178	60.5
1982	38.5	294	209	174	59.2
1987	39.3	294	213	187	63.6
1991	36.9	294	213	189	64.3
1996	37.9	294	217	157	53.4
Naveen Patnaik – Biju Janata Dal (BJD), Odisha					
2000	29.4	147	84	68	46.3

Year	Vote Share (%)	Seats			Win Rate (%)
		Total	Contested	Won	
2004	27.4	147	84	61	41.5
2009	38.9	147	129	103	70.1
2014	43.4	147	147	117	79.6
2019	44.7	147	146	112	76.2

Sources: Election Commission of India; author's calculations
Notes: (1) National Vote Share is the vote share obtained in that election.
(2) Win Rate is the percentage of seats won to seats contested.

How comparable are Modi's national wins to Nehru's?

Table 3.2 compares Nehru's wins (three) to Modi's (two to date). It is a split decision – Modi is behind in vote shares, but marginally ahead in wins (as per cent of seats contested). The win rates are close – Nehru 65.7% across three elections, Modi 67.7%; vote shares – Modi 34.1% versus 45.8% for Nehru. Modi's peak vote share is more than 10 percentage points behind Nehru in his second 1957 election.

Table 3.2: Modi vs Nehru – Performance as Prime Minister

Year	National Vote Share (%)	Seats		Win Rate (%)
		Contested	Won	
Nehru				
1952	45.0	479	299	62.4
1957	47.8	490	298	60.8
1962	44.7	488	361	74.0

Year	National Vote Share (%)	Seats		Win Rate (%)
		Contested	Won	
Modi				
2014	31.0	428	282	65.9
2019	37.3	436	303	69.5

Sources: Election Commission of India; author's calculations
Notes: (1) National Vote Share is the vote share obtained in that election.
(2) Win Rate is the percentage of seats won to seats contested.

But the world was very different then. No Opposition, low literacy, no social media, low Index of Opposition Unity (IOU). It is not sufficiently appreciated that at the time of Independence, the average educational attainment in India was less than two years.

In the early Independence years, for the electorate, the There Is No Alternative (TINA) factor dominated. And for an ex-colonial poor and largely illiterate economy, it was TINA squared. In terms of seats, Nehru obtained around 350 seats in the three elections (1952, 1957 and 1962). What is clear is he did not win because of economic performance or because of bold policy initiatives. Indeed, most of the post-Nehru–Indira Gandhi period has been consumed by political leaders wanting to change the course of India's economy and development.

Nehru and early India's economic record

At the time of India's independence, the world was emerging out of the double whammy of the Depression and World War II. Nehru's three terms yielded an average per capita growth of 0.6%. It is commonly believed that the international economic climate was heavily oriented towards state intervention, planning and socialism.

This was not the case. More accurately, the reality was a Cold War divide, with developing countries and its non-aligned leaders clearly preferring the example of the Soviet Union rather than that of Japan, Europe or the US. To be sure, even the West was leaning towards more state intervention, but this was along 'liberal' Keynesian lines rather than the draconian Soviet methods. However, Asian economies, excluding the countries in South Asia and China, preferred the Western model of growth with less government control and more economic freedom.

It is difficult to overestimate the influence of the 'get industrialized quick' model of the Soviet Union on the Indian leaders. As early as 1948, the Congress party adopted the Industrial Policy Resolution, a policy document that was to become a formal part of Indian Planning, as annexure to the Approach paper to the Second Plan in 1956. In 1950, the Constitution of India came into being, and it contained an important section called 'Directive Principles'. These principles did not have force of law – for example, the state could not be sued if the promise of universal primary education was not met (one of the Directive Principles). But the state was directed to adopt policies which would enhance the direction of these Principles. And the setting up of the Planning Commission was explicitly in accordance to the Directive Principles.

The sequence of events/thinking leading to India being a socialist state, in word and deed, was as follows. First, as cited in Granville, Austin, *The Indian Constitution: Cornerstone of a Nation* (Oxford University Press, 1999):

> the content of the [Congress] party's *socialism* became clear in its 1931 Karachi Resolution. Among other things, it said that 'key industries and services, mineral resources, railways, waterways [and] shipping' were to be government controlled, and the government was to safeguard the interests of 'industrial workers' and women and children . . . The *Congress Socialist Party – formed in 1934 –* of which Nehru was a supportive non-member supported a policy of 'elimination of princes and landlords and all other classes of exploiters without *compensation* and 'redistribution of land to peasants' [emphases added].

These issues found their way into the discussions of the Constituent Assembly, and later the Constitution itself. Indeed, the much reviled bank nationalization of Indira Gandhi was contained in the Industrial Disputes Act of 1947, an act which includes a list of industries that could be declared public in the interests of the state or development. Second on the list was 'banking', third was cement, fourth was coal, fifth was cotton textiles, sixth was foodstuffs, seventh was iron and steel. The fact that even foodstuffs and textiles were contained in a list of activities to be nationalized makes a mockery of the belief that the public sector was 'forced' to step in because the private sector was unwilling. This was control at its zenith, and with substantially less economic freedom than what the Indian public had ever experienced.

That Nehru was a Fabian socialist is well known, but the general impression remains that he did not let these sentiments affect policymaking. The Constitution, which contains his personal stamp, does not provide for much economic freedom. Intervention is writ large. Both in ideology and deed, Nehru was more than an armchair socialist. This should come as a surprise given India had greater economic freedom prior to, and during, the colonial era, than it did at the dawn of its political independence.

And this was what Nehru stated in 1958 after his economic doctrine as contained in the Second Five Year Plan, 1956–61: 'Socialism to some people means two things: Distribution which means cutting off the pockets of the people who have too much money and nationalization. Both these are *desirable* objectives' [emphasis added].

A dispassionate look at Nehru's foreign policy record also throws up several missteps. For example, giving up a UN Security Council seat to China, being betrayed by China in the 1962 war after all of India was chanting 'Hindi–Chini

Bhai Bhai' for several years. His failed economic record is one of unabashed state control of the economy.

Modi's record as chief minister of Gujarat

A large part of this book is about Modi's record as PM over the last ten years. My contribution to the volume *Modi@20 – Dreams Meet Delivery* discussed Modi's Gujarat record in some detail. Table 3.3 outlines his economic record in two dimensions – growth and poverty.

Table 3.3: Performance of Gujarat Versus Other Big States, 1992–2012 (%)

| | | | | Excess Growth Gujarat | |
	Big States	Comparable States	Gujarat	Big States	Comparable
Per Capita GDP Growth					
Period 1 (1992–2001)	2.9	3.7	3.4	0.5	-0.3
Period 2 (2003–2012)	6.2	6.5	7.9	1.7	1.4
Extreme Poverty Change (All)					
Period 1 (1993–1999)	-3.9	-8.5	-1.8	2.1	6.7
Period 2 (1999–2011)	-18.3	-16.7	-19.6	-1.3	-2.9
Extreme Poverty Change (SC+ST)					
Period 1 (1993–1999)	-4.0	-10.8	5.8	9.8	16.6
Period 2 (1999–2011)	-24.1	-23.3	-27.9	-3.8	-4.6

	Big States	Comparable States	Gujarat	Excess Growth Gujarat	
				Big States	Comparable
Extreme Poverty change (Muslims)					
Period 1 (1993–1999)	-8.5	-6.5	-3.6	4.9	2.9
Period 2 (1999–2011)	-21.4	-28.2	-28.1	-6.7	0.1

Source: Surjit S. Bhalla, Chapter 3, 'Success of People-Centric Approach', in *Modi@20: Dreams Meet Delivery.*

Notes: (1) Period 1 is when Modi is not CM of Gujarat; Period 2 is when he is CM of Gujarat.

(2) Extreme Poverty is defined as poverty according to the Tendulkar poverty line (also $1.9 in 2011 PPP).

(3) All rates are averages of annual per cent changes; poverty change is in terms of change in per cent poor.

(4) Comparable states are Haryana, Kerala, Maharashtra, Punjab and Tamil Nadu.

There appears to be a strong reason why Modi has likely the most exceptional state record across three dimensions – vote shares, seat shares and growth. The table discusses Gujarat's record for two decades – the pre-Modi-in-Gujarat period 1992–2001 and the Modi-in-Gujarat period 2003–12.

A multi-dimensional performance table is presented to answer most queries of readers: How did Gujarat perform with respect to other big states? And within big states, how did Gujarat perform with respect to high-flying growth-poverty reduction states like Haryana, Kerala, Maharashtra, Punjab and Tamil Nadu?

It does not matter what metric is used. Gujarat had close to zero excess GDP growth in the pre-Modi decade; with Modi, 1.5% plus extra growth. Poverty reduction – Gujarat performed worse than other states in the pre-Modi years; Modi years saw a much better performance. Of particular interest are the last two rows in the model – how have Muslims in Gujarat fared? According to the Tendulkar poverty line, poverty reduction for Muslims was much larger when Modi was present than when he was not.

As we will show in the rest of the chapters, Modi's record-breaking economic performance has now translated into exceptional performance across time and within India, and in comparison to other countries.

Does the exceptional Modi record provide a perspective on the Congress record of singling out Modi for exceptional targeting? Was it the case that the Congress ecosystem realized early on that Modi would be a formidable challenger to the throne of the dynasty? The Godhra riots did happen, and have been often stated as provocation, and reason, for Congress's antipathy to Modi, the denial of US visa via the ecosystem, and descriptions like *Maut ka Saudagar* (merchant of death). But the Sikh riots did happen under the Congress, and less people have been punished for the Delhi riots than for Godhra, and a long and proper investigation has taken place under the monitoring of the court in the Godhra riots, but no such effort was made by the Congress for the 1984 riots in Delhi.

Growing up in independent India (I am a Midnight's Child, circa 1948), and under a heavily pro-Congress regime in just-independent India, I remember the descriptions and attacks by the ecosystem on anyone who was not Congress. The Rashtriya Swayamsevak Sangh (RSS) was particularly singled out for attack, as were those who disagreed with the Nehru–Gandhi Congress on economic or social policies. All one heard growing up was the Congress narrative on economic and social policies, and the rejection and ridicule of anyone providing a different perspective.

The dynasty's approach has been to take no political prisoners; if not a Nehru–Gandhi, then you are not Congress and not to be favoured. Let there be no competition for leadership. What other explanation is there to explain the treatment of one of the tallest leaders of the Congress party, Narasimha Rao?

4

The Democracy in Democracies[1]

Common Era 2024 is a bumper year for elections worldwide. The Covid years, 2020 and 2021, were witness to democratic backsliding around the world, especially in Western economies that had been heretofore insulated from occasional democratic backsliding, a norm in most of the world. The concept of democracy backsliding involves the erosion of democratic norms, institutions and values, and it has gained prominence in the discourse around political developments globally.

It is also the age of polarization, and this is reflected in the time trend of some of the popular variables that attempt to measure 'democracy'. What polarization does is exaggerate and embellish the point of view of those giving their subjective views in an 'objective' manner. Hence, the popularity of the view that democracy is backsliding, a view that obtained a significant leg-up after Brexit and the installation of the Trump presidency. These backsliding narratives are deeply entrenched in the beliefs of the

Western world and the old elite. Academic circles, too, have embraced this description.

The time trend for 'democracy' for India is suggestive, according to some 'experts', of backsliding. In a working paper titled 'Why India Does Poorly on Global Perception Indices', Sanyal and Arora (2022) take three indices used by the popular and the authoritative World Bank's World Governance Indicators (WGI).

The three indices (among several) used in the construction of the WGI are Freedom House's (FH's) Freedom in the World Index, Economist Intelligence Unit (EIU) Democracy Index and the Varieties of Democracy (V-DEM) indices – these are important and widely followed indices. Sanyal and Arora conclude negatively on the usefulness of the democracy indices: 'A common thread in all these indices is that they are derived from the perceptions or opinions of few experts. These institutions do not provide any transparency on how the experts were chosen or even their expertise or nationality (except in the case of V-DEM where they clarify that they chose some experts from each country from different fields).'[2] They also raise concerns over the questionnaire design by saying, 'A reading of the questionnaire shows that most of the questions are subjective in nature, hence simply providing the same questions for all countries does not mean getting comparable scores for different countries as the generic questions can be answered very differently by experts.'

These subjective readings are the basis of important policy decisions. Sanyal and Arora point out that these rankings have concrete implications, especially for developing economies. For instance, these indices are inputs into the World Bank's WGI that, in turn, have approximately 18–20% weightage in sovereign ratings. The WGI has about 385 different indicators from more than 30 different data sources, including FH, V-DEM, etc.

We examine the WGI in some detail in this chapter. As mentioned earlier, it uses the FH index as one of its inputs into the construction of its six component variables. In 1991, as part of the World Bank's World Development Report [WDR] 1991, *The Challenge of Development,* I used FH's index of political and civil liberties for my chapter on 'The Paths to Development'. At that time, FH was the only democracy variable available. Daniel Kaufman, one of the two authors behind the construction of the WGI, was my colleague on the WDR report led by Vinod Thomas.

This background is provided for two reasons – one, for our preference in using the two indices – FH and WGI – to examine trends in democracy in India (and the rest of the world); second, to illustrate how this sensitive subjective issue was handled in less polarized times.

I used the FH index to show that there was a marked correlation between economic growth and the presence of political and civil liberties. Prior to this report, the World Bank had steered clear of any 'political' discussion in its reports. Lawrence Summers was the chief economist at the bank, and he represented and supported the WDR team's view that 'freedom' could not be separated from concerns about development. Ernie Stern, the senior-most vice president at the bank, first demurred but later enthusiastically supported this 'non-economic' but not non-developmental addition to the Report.

Thirty years later, the construction of democracy indices is more than a cottage industry – the indices have become weapons of polarized ideology. India, along with many other democracies, has become a poster child of the 'democracy backsliding' narrative. Almost all the major news providers of the 'old world' have covered this as a front page lead at some point in the last ten years (see *Financial Times [FT]*, Chatham House, *Foreign Affairs*, *Democracy Journal*, V-DEM). These concerns have inspired efforts such as 'Democracy Erosion', a website that describes itself as 'a consortium of researchers, students, policymakers, and practitioners committed to marshalling evidence and learning to address the growing crisis of democratic erosion worldwide'. In a series of posts on India, Sklar (2020) and Ozturk (2021) squarely attribute the cause of democratic erosion in India to Prime Minister Modi.

However, it is important to note that all the empirical evidence for the website judgements has come from subjective expert scores produced by various research and policy institutes (which are predictably of a certain age and ideological bent). A recent paper by Little and Meng (2023, henceforth L&M), 'Measuring Democratic Backsliding', threw a spanner in the ideology by calling into question this global narrative saying, 'While the overall pattern of democratic backsliding is based primarily on subjective evaluation by experts, objective evidence on this trend is lacking . . . Survey objective indicators of democracy – such as incumbent performance in elections – find little evidence of global democratic decline over the last decade. While we cannot rule out the possibility that the world is experiencing major democratic backsliding exclusively in ways which require subjective judgement to detect, this claim is not justified by existing evidence.'[3]

They go on to hypothesize, using data from Google Scholar and other databases of media events, that '. . . there is evidence of increased media and scholarly attention to democratic erosion. Given this increase is much more dramatic than even subjective measures of democratic backsliding, it is hard to not infer the trend is at least partially driven by more intense media coverage of these events.'

The first and most frequently used data set was developed by the NGO Freedom House and currently covers 195 countries (Freedom House 2019). This data set measures variables that are not necessarily components of democracy, including corruption, civilian police control, violent crimes, willingness to grant political asylum and the right to buy and sell land (Coppedge et al. 2011). The report's methodology is derived in large measure from the Universal Declaration of Human Rights, adopted by the UN General Assembly in 1948. To produce annual democracy scores, FH holds meetings with expert analysts to reach a consensus on country-level scores.

As this is a book on elections, we believe most readers would be familiar with the idea of 'poll-of-polls' when there are multiple polls from multiple pollsters for any given election. Similarly, a wide variety of democracy measures are in use today, from large-scale, continuously updated indices maintained by large organizations (such as the ones mentioned above) to boutique efforts by individual researchers for particular projects. As one might expect, while these measures are typically highly correlated, they still differ significantly for some countries and years. Such differences are both conceptual (researchers disagree about the essential characteristics of democracy) and empirical (researchers disagree about whether a given country-year is democratic according to a particular definition). Lueders and Lust (2018) show that there is considerable disagreement between the various democracy data sets, which underscores the subjective nature of these scores.

Since FH and WGI are the two oldest, the best and the least biased (in our view) of the subjective indices on democracy, we decided to explore the trends in these two variables for all the countries. Both indices use a variety of sources as inputs into their ranking. The WGI, for example, uses 385 indicators from a variety of data sources (see Table 4.1).

Table 4.1: Number of Indicators in WGI by Data Source

Data Source	Number of Indicators
Institutional Profiles Database (IPD)	59
World Economic Forum Global Competitiveness Survey (GCS)	37
Institute for Management Development World Competitiveness Yearbook (WCY)	30
Economist Intelligence Unit (EIU)	26
Global Integrity Index (GII)	24
IHS MARKIT (WMO)	24
AFR	16
Bertelsmann Transformation Index (BTI)	15
Business Environment and Enterprise Performance Survey (BPS)	15
Latinobarometro (LBO)	15
Freedom House (FH)	12
IFAD Rural Sector Performance Assessments (IFD)	12
Political Risk Services International Country Risk Guide (PRS)	10
Transparency International Global Corruption Barometer (GCB)	10
Other Miscellaneous Sources (18 sources)	80
Total	385

Source: World Bank World Governance Indicators (WGI)
Notes: Overall, the WGI comprises 385 indicators from 32 data sources as inputs. Data sources with more than 10 or more indicators are reported in the table.

Our approach to understanding trends in democracy rankings is a multi-step procedure:

Step 1: Take the six indicators in the WGI and compute a composite rank of ranks (using a Borda ranking system for the statistically inclined). The six indicators are Voice and Accountability, Political Stability and Absence of Violence/ Terrorism, Government Effectiveness, Regulatory Quality, Rule of Law, and Control of Corruption. Conveniently and usefully, the WGI provides the percentile ranking of the six indices, besides the absolute value of the six indices. This allows the WGI rankings to be used as a ranking of performance.

Step 2: Take the FH composite indicator (also a composite of the indices they use) and compute a super-composite ranking of broadly defined 'Democracy'. In other words, take the two ranks – the WGI composite rank and the FH composite rank – add them, and then rank the addition in reverse order. This way the best (most democratic) is ranked as number one. This is the Borda rank.

Three tables, 4.2, 4.3 and 4.4, contain our experiments with democracy indices. Table 4.2 contains the levels of the three indices – FH, WGI and Composite.

These indices are estimates made at specific points in time. The interpretation is that a lower number (rank closer to 1) is a 'better' democracy. The change in these indices between 2004 and 2022 is what will give us an 'answer' as to how each country has performed between 2004 and 2022.

Table 4.2: Democracy Indicators Ranking – Selected Countries

Country	FH 2004	FH 2022	World Governance Indicators 2004	World Governance Indicators 2022	WGI and FH Composite Rank 2004	WGI and FH Composite Rank 2022
Bangladesh	125	139	179	168	151	153
Brazil	86	80	104	129	94	104
France	24	47	33	43	28	45
India	86	93	119	112	102	102
Indonesia	114	93	155	111	134	102
Korea	55	63	59	45	56	53
Mexico	71	107	104	146	87	126
Pakistan	161	139	172	168	166	153
Philippines	86	107	137	128	111	117
Singapore	136	120	27	22	81	71
Sri Lanka	100	120	116	138	108	128
Turkey	100	151	109	144	104	147
UK	24	22	28	32	25	26
US	24	63	37	48	30	55

Source: FH, World Bank, World Governance Indicators; author's calculations
Notes:
(1) WGI reports both raw numbers as well as percentiles for the indicators. Only percentiles are used in this analysis.
(2) The six different indicators of democracy in WGI which are combined into one rank using Borda rank method.
(3) Composite Rank is the rank average of the two indices; a lower rank means better democracy.

A negative number is indicative of backsliding. Prominent in this regard are five countries, starting with the most backsliding: Turkey, Mexico, the US, Sri Lanka and France. Each reader can form her own judgement but we were surprised with the large backsliding in Mexico. By our method, Indonesia is the most improved democracy in this set – its composite rank moved from 134 to 102. Pakistan also improved – from a much lower 166 in 2004 to a somewhat improved 153. It still is the least democratic country on our list, marginally worse than Turkey in 2022.

We started our discussion with the expectation that the composite index would show backsliding in India. India's change between 2004 and 2022 is zero; our method suggests no backsliding. The WGI shows an improvement and the FH index an equal and opposite deterioration in the ranks. In both cases, the change is small, compared to the larger changes in the other countries.

Table 4.3: Change in Democracy Indicator Rankings, 2004–2022

Country	FH	WGI	Composite
Bangladesh	14	-11	2
Brazil	-6	25	10
France	23	10	17
India	7	-7	0
Indonesia	-21	-44	-32
Korea	8	-14	-3
Mexico	36	42	39
Pakistan	-22	-4	-13
Philippines	21	-9	6
Singapore	-16	-5	-10
Sri Lanka	20	22	20

Country	FH	WGI	Composite
Turkey	51	35	43
UK	-2	4	1
US	39	11	25

Source: FH, World Bank, WGI; author's calculations

Notes:

1) Each cell represents the change from 2004 to 2002 for each country in each of the indices.
2) Minus sign for a change in index indicates an improvement.

V-DEM and EIU

Table 4.4 offers a composite rank of two other composite indices – a composite index formed from the seven component indices contained in V-DEM. The EIU represents the index constructed by the Economist Intelligence Unit. These two units are provided for a comparison and a hint about the volatile time trends in these indices. For example, V-DEM appears to be a very volatile indicator with much larger changes when compared to other countries. In contrast to FH, which showed the US rank declining by 39 and the WGI rank declining by 11, V-DEM indicates a broadly steady nature of democracy for the US. And France, a prominent backslider in FH, shows virtually no change over time in either V-DEM or EIU.

Table 4.4: V-DEM and EIU Rankings – Selected Countries

	V-DEM		EIU		Change	
	2004	*2022*	*2006*	*2022*	*VDEM*	*EIU*
Bangladesh	114	139	76	73	-25	3
Brazil	29	65	42	51	-36	-9
France	13	13	24	23	0	1
India	52	104	35	47	-52	-12
Indonesia	58	76	66	54	-18	12
Korea	26	29	31	24	-3	7
Mexico	62	79	53	89	-17	-36
Pakistan	119	111	114	107	8	7
Philippines	90	101	64	52	-11	12
Singapore	109	101	84	70	8	14
Sri Lanka	94	80	57	60	14	-3
Turkey	62	133	88	103	-71	-15
UK	23	21	23	18	2	5
US	23	29	17	30	-6	-13

Sources: V-DEM, EIU; author's calculations

Notes: (1) 2006 is the first available year for EIU therefore we present 2006 ranks and change between 2022 and 2006.

(2) Minus sign for a change in index indicates an improvement.

To summarize, some of the major results are the following (based on FH, WGI and Composite).

(1) India's rank in 2004 was 102, and it obtained the same rank in 2022. No slide here.

(2) France, Sri Lanka, Turkey and the US reveal a significant amount of democratic backsliding.

(3) The most improved democracy is Indonesia (in this 14-country set), with a 32 jump in rank. The worst performers are Mexico and Turkey.

(4) Pakistan held the lowest rank in 2004 and 2022, but its rank has improved by 13 points over the last two decades.

As we discussed earlier in this chapter, we are not fans of democracy indices in the present polarized-ideological age. Hence, we chose, for illustrative purposes, the two indices we are relatively most comfortable with. We also presented two other popular indices of democracy – V-DEM and EIU.

The results are all over the place. We leave it to the readers to form their own judgements (and encourage them to do their own analysis). But what we want to emphasize is that there is little evidence according to two broad indices of democratic backsliding in India.

5

Majority Rule and Minority Experience[1]

Democracy is both about majority rule and minority rights. All minorities, no matter where in the world, and no matter what religion, at some point feel that they are being discriminated against.

It is important that minorities feel secure and have equal rights. But what happens when a society bends 'too much' to accommodate the rights of minorities, be it because of religion, sex, caste or sexual orientation? In the constitutional debates, there was healthy disagreement on how to tackle 'forever discrimination' against the Dalits. No one disagreed with the goal that some policy *must* be enacted. India chose the command economy route of quota reservations rather than the more liberal, and secular, route of affirmative action.

The demand for a caste census is just the latest manifestation of a policy gone awry. How awry? As in the Supreme Court interpretation of quotas: there is a 50% cap on the quota for reservations, but the quota is very elastic. At times, it can be more than 50%. Our policymakers and/

or their advisers, and even our lawmakers, forever think that people are stupid; if you think that the description is extreme, substitute 'irrational' for stupid. Sometime back, I had stated that the anti-liberal, anti-secular, anti-merit system would end only when everyone demanded reservation. Yesterday, the Jats wanted reservations; today, it is the Marathas; tomorrow it will be the Brahmins. Just you wait!

Well, wait no longer. The Bihar census yielded the following estimates (never mind that the implied fertility rates of some castes may be beyond comprehension or reality).

Different Castes and Communities (Bihar)	Population (%)
Extremely Backward Classes (EBCs)	36.01
Other Backward Classes (OBCs)	27.12
Scheduled Castes (SCs)	19.65
Scheduled Tribes (STs)	1.68
Buddhists, Christians, Sikhs and Jains	< 1
Total Population (Bihar)	13.07 crore

Source: Bihar Caste Census 2023

But count you must: SCs and STs 21%; EBCs 36%; OBCs 27%. Since all of the above deserve reservations (a total of 85%), we are as close to 100% reservation as we will ever get.

One of the accepted beliefs about Modi's tenure as PM is that he was chief minister of Gujarat at the time the

Godhra riots happened, and therefore he, and his policies, are likely to be discriminatory towards Muslims.

We saw in Chapter 3 how official consumer survey data conducted by the National Sample Survey Office (NSSO) showed that the welfare of poor Muslims in Gujarat had improved at least as fast as of those who were not Muslim. And welfare of Muslims had increased faster in Gujarat than in other states. The Modi government has increased welfare spending via direct benefit transfer (DBT) schemes and provided free grain to all; it is now conventional wisdom that free food and DBT do not discriminate on the basis of caste or religion.

Economics of discrimination in India (Muslims) and the US (blacks)

Opinions come cheap, and everyone is entitled to an opinion. George Soros has been openly critical of 'democracy' in India and predicted its imminent decline, and former President Obama added his weight to Soros's opinion by stating that 'if you do not protect the rights of ethnic minorities in India, then there is a strong possibility that India at some point starts pulling apart'.[2] That President Obama said this when the floodlights were on Mr Modi (before his speech to a joint session of the US Congress on 23 June 2023) added fuel to the Soros fire.

Obama joins a long list of scholars and politicians

predicting a Balkanization, if not imminent demise, of the Indian state. Way back in the 1960s, Selig Harrison warned that unless a new democratic leader arose post Nehru, 'India will face Balkanization or authoritarian control based on army force'.[3]

Obama's comment is a more judicious rephrasing of Mr Harrison's 'forecast' some sixty years ago. Closer to home, former RBI Governor Raghuram Rajan recently stated, 'We must confront and defeat majoritarian authoritarianism. Any attempt to make 2nd class citizens of our minority (read Muslim) population will not lead us anywhere.'[4]

These assertions have a logical basis. There are more Muslims in India than in any other country in the world barring Indonesia. How Muslims and any other minority (lower castes and tribals and women for that matter) are treated is of immense importance to the stability of India, its progress and its well-being. As has been correctly asserted by many (including myself), India's strength is in its diversity, and some of us have asserted (and empirically shown) that India, despite all gloom and doom forecasts, has survived in large part as a democratic nation because of electoral diversity, which allows for effective checks and balances.

Empirical conclusions are difficult on this sensitive, emotive subject because it is tough to establish that a community has been penalized by discrimination or racism. Prejudice is multifaceted. Economists, not surprisingly, have taken an empirical approach with Nobel laureate Gary Becker setting the standard, and the trend, with his 1957 study *The Economics of Discrimination*. Becker's point was very simple – if measured properly, discrimination was unlikely to exist without racism (or casteism or sexism).

By Becker's definition (now accepted by all), wage incomes are primarily a function of education, experience and inherent ability. Ability is difficult to measure, but considerable progress in measurement has occurred. The simple Becker conclusion: Those who practise discrimination in the marketplace will make *less profits* because they will be hiring *less productive* (white in the US context) workers at a higher wage. In other words, to measure the contribution of racism, look at the wage differential between whites and blacks *after* accounting for differences in human capital.

The study of wage differentials constitutes just one approach to recognizing discrimination. There are many methods or empirical strategies to establish how well a minority is protected (or unprotected) in different countries. Hence, a direct evaluation of the veracity of the Obama statement (Hindu prejudice against Muslims) is not straightforward.

The extensive study on black–white wage differentials in the US provides a useful approach. It has been a prolific industry in the US since the Becker publication and, for the last 30-odd years, has also been extended to sex discrimination. American audiences are very aware of this research, and any study of discrimination in India or elsewhere has to compare and contrast it with the American findings.

If there were no discrimination, after controlling for human capital, one would expect blacks and whites to have similar earnings (wages). Analogously, if Muslims were discriminated against, then some amount of this bias would occur in their earnings, i.e. Muslims would have lower average earnings than Hindus. This is what we do – compare black and white differences in earnings, and the differences in Hindu and Muslim earnings.

Wage discrimination and inequality in India and the US

Discrimination can take many forms. Inclusion and non-inclusion can take many forms. One less studied aspect of wage inequality is that between communities such as Hindus and Muslims. We do that below. Data from NSSO/PLFS (Periodic Labour Force Survey) studies (1983 to 2022) have been assembled. Wages of all workers, including self-employed, are available since 2017; for years prior, only data on salaried (formal sector workers) and casual (informal sector workers) are available.

Table 5.1 contains the data for the period 1983 to 2022 on wage gaps for male Hindus and Muslims, Whites and blacks. For the US, the data and results are obtained from the Valerie Wilson and William Darity, Jr study (2022) for the Economic Policy Institute; for India, we use earnings data from the NSSO/PLFS studies conducted since 1983.

For the US, Wilson-Darity conclude:

> Another defining feature of racial inequality in the labor market is the significant pay disparities between black and white workers. In 2019, the typical (median) black worker earned 24.4% less per hour than the typical white worker. This is an even larger wage gap than in 1979, when it was 16.4%. Controlling for racial differences in education, experience, and the fact that black workers are more likely to live in lower-wage Southern states leaves an unexplained gap of 14.9% in 2019 (out of a total average gap of 26.5%).[5]

What is noteworthy about the US data is that despite consistent and persistent attention to the elimination of discrimination, black males still earned about 25% less than white males in 2022 (median wages). And that since 1983, there has not been much improvement; likely, some deterioration.

The data for the raw differences in the medians earnings of Muslim and Hindus are also reported in the table. In addition, for India, is the earnings gap between Hindus and Muslims *after* controlling for differences in human capital. No matter what index is chosen, there is no evidence of Muslims earning less than Hindus, *ceteris paribus.* In the last year reported, 2022–23, PLFS data, the median Muslim earnings were about 18% more than median Hindu earnings.

Thus, in striking contrast to the US, and against the 'expectations' of many, Muslims have not encountered wage discrimination in the labour market in India. The wage gap has moved towards equalization – from a *positive* 10% in 1983 to a positive 18% in 2022 (in favour of Muslims).

Table 5.1: Religion and Race Wage Gaps in India and the US

Year	Male Median Real Wage (₹)		Male Median Real Wage Ratios (%)		
	Muslim	Hindu	Muslim/ Hindu	Muslim/ Hindu, After Controlling for Human Capital	US Black/ White Median Wage Ratio
1983	1718	1558	110.3	100.0	81.7
1993	2446	2327	105.1	91.9	80.2
1999	2941	2694	109.2	94.3	80.4
2004	2814	2887	97.5	91.7	80.1
2011	4393	4519	97.2	92.3	77.8
2017	5871	5871	100.0	101.8	74.7
2021	6299	6205	101.5	103.4	76.6
2022	7538	6408	117.6	103.1	78.5

Sources: NSSO and PLFS data; EPI data for the US
Note: Male Real Earnings in 2011–12 prices, ₹ per month; from 2017–18 onwards, real median earnings include those from self-employment; human capital controlled for via Oaxaca-Blinder decomposition; US data from Wilson-Darity (2022); wage gap defined as wage relative to Hindus, whites.

Also offered is a more refined version of measuring discrimination. Wages are a function of human capital (endowments), and one needs to adjust for differences in human capital to find out the net effect. The net result: Muslims were 10% ahead in 1983 and 1% ahead in 2021, after controlling for differences in human capital.

Wage discrimination is not the only form of discrimination. However, it is reassuring to know that, on one important dimension, we are not practising what Soros or Obama thought we might be doing. Societies practise prejudice and discrimination in many ways. According to Pew surveys, both Hindus and Muslims want to live peacefully but separately.

Families do not want inter-caste marriages; they do not want interfaith marriages. Families prefer not to have large disparities in husband–wife incomes or of family background. Progress comes via the dismantling of these prejudices, and progress does not come easy. Hence, it is always preferable not to get judgemental.

The polemics of judgements

But it is hard to avoid harsh judgements. I want to relate an exchange between a respected Indian intellectual, B.R. Shenoy, and a respected Muslim intellectual from Pakistan, and former finance minister, Shahid Javed Burki. I am privileged to 'know' both these individuals; Mr Burki was my senior colleague during my time at the World Bank in the 1980s, and Mr Shenoy here in India.

Mr Burki published an article in the *Express Tribune* in 2024 entitled 'The Story of the Other India'.[6] Much like the narratives I have talked about in this book, Mr Burki's narrative was that 'Muslims are downgraded to a second class status by Modi and the ruling party, BJP'. Mr Shenoy then provided the following facts about the status, rights, etc., of Hindus and Muslims in India. I am paraphrasing and reproducing Mr Shenoy's response to Mr Burki's article (with his permission).

Fact: Indian Muslims enjoy more constitutional rights than the Hindus, such as conversions to Islam of Hindus, right to education, owning property, marriages, religious teachings in schools and colleges etc.

Also note that in India:

1. The government/s exercise no control on mosques, dargahs, mazars etc., while all Hindu temples are under the control of the respective state governments;

2. In South of India, all temple collections (amounting to Rs. thousands of crores per annum) become part of government treasury, while not a paisa is taken from any mosque.

3. The governments fund Islamic studies in madrassas. The University Grants Commission (UGC) permits colleges and schools to have departments teaching

Islamic theology, whereas teaching Hindu Theology is illegal!

4. Muslim men can marry 4 times, legally, whereas Hindu men cannot marry even a second time!

5. From 1951 to 2011 (60 years) people following Indian Religions (defined as religions that originated in India such as Sikh, Buddhist and Jain as well as Hindu) increased their numbers by 3.2 times (from 31.5 cr to 101 cr), while the Muslim population during the same period multiplied by 5.5 times (from 3.7 cr to 20 cr)! **During the same period, Hindu and Sikh population in Pakistan, unsurprisingly, has almost disappeared!**

6. Next to the GOI and the Indian Railways, WAQF boards are the biggest land owners! No Hindu is appointed as administrators or CEOs to these Waqf Boards, whereas Muslims and Christians are routinely appointed by state governments to administer Hindu temples including the holiest Hindu temples in Tirupati, Guruvayur, Vaishno Devi etc.!

7. While the Directive Principles prefacing the Indian Constitution desire Uniform Civil Code to be enacted for governing the personal laws of the whole of the Indian community, Nehru enacted Hindu Code Bill in 1955 but left the Muslim community untouched, much against the express opinion of Dr Ambedkar!

Much maligned though Modi is, there has been no decrease in the benefits of his socio-economic reforms going to the Muslim community. Poor Muslims have equally benefited from government largesse like free toilets, free houses, free monthly rations, free power, gas, health insurance, scholarships and many other benefits.

6

Democratic Backsliding in India – Some Narrative 'Evidence'[1]

Along with a narrative of the decline of 'Opinion Democracy in India' (Chapter 4) and the narrative of internal democracy in India (Chapter 5), we now have 'evidence' of voter manipulation in India, provided by Dr Sabyasachi Das, when he was Assistant Professor at the Ashoka University.

Sabyasachi Das published a paper whose findings can best be described (sympathetically) as unsubstantiated. Its release on social media in its pre-review stage, ostensibly without even any feedback process in university circles, is highly unusual (even unprecedented) and suggests the targeting of an international echo chamber sympathetic to the cause of unearthing 'Democratic Backsliding' in the Indian polity.

In addition, the paper garnered attention due to its clickbait claims of voter manipulation by the BJP during the 2019 parliamentary elections in India. Sabyasachi Das entered this debate by positioning his analysis as a response to Little and Meng's (2023) recent paper 'Measuring

Democratic Backsliding'. Little and Meng had muddied the narrative waters by calling the narrative of Democracy Decline across the world into question by saying, 'Democratic backsliding is a hugely important topic, and we believe that it is crucial to provide an accurate depiction of the current state of the world. As others have already noted, *expert-coded measures* document only a weak decline in recent years. We add to this observation that on objective indicators there is minimal evidence of global backsliding. Of course, we are not claiming that backsliding is not occurring in any particular country. But if the world really is experiencing major backsliding in the aggregate, we should expect to see some evidence of this on objective measures' [emphasis added and note the reference to coding].[2]

In the introduction to his paper, Das states, 'I contribute to this important debate by examining objective evidence of democratic backsliding in the form of electoral manipulation in the world's largest democracy – India.'[3] The *objective* evidence is described by Das as emanating directly from democratic behaviour as opposed to indirect evidence supplied by broad indices as provided by global indices like V-DEM and FH, etc. The question remains – how strong is the direct evidence of undemocratic (electoral fraud) behaviour provided by Das – a matter investigated prominently by @Saiarav (referring to their username on X/ Twitter; he also goes by Yajnavalkya on Medium), Kapoor (2023)[4] and us.

To put it mildly, Das's paper was a 'sensation' when it first appeared via X on Indian political screens. Allegations of voter fraud or ballot stuffing or registration hurdles for those the ruling regime considers unfriendly occur before, during and after every election in India. That is a dog bites man story.

What Das offers is a woman bites dog story. In particular, that by applying a strict statistical test, there is, for the first time in Indian electoral history, statistical evidence of voting fraud. This statistical test has been examined for the US (Vogl 2011)[5] and found wanting. Indeed, it is very rare for voting behaviour anywhere to yield the statistical result of voter result tampering.

The statistical test that Das uses is called the McCrary Test. The intuitive idea behind the test is to look for discontinuities in patterns of voting behaviour. But what is a discontinuity in the pattern? A heuristic explanation is as follows. BJP won 303 seats out of 436 it contested in 2019 to yield a high win percentage of 69.5%. A high percentage of wins is not a problem in itself – after all the Congress won 82% of seats it contested in 1984. So what is the question or the problem? The margin of wins was not 'evenly distributed' around the 0% margin range in close contests, where a close contest is defined as plus or minus 5%. Building on this shaky statistical foundation, Das had contended that a significant jump in the density of BJP win margins near zero in BJP-ruled states had led him to believe that the BJP had a higher likelihood of winning closely contested seats compared to other parties. Das concluded, and we paraphrase, that such a failure of the McCrary Test was rare, that it was observed only in the 2019 elections in India and none in the previous general elections for either the BJP or the Congress, or for state assembly elections held simultaneously with the 2019 general election or for those held *subsequently*.

Further, Das looks for possibilities of electoral manipulation by the BJP in the 2019 election and finds evidence that the McCrary Test fails *only* in BJP-ruled states – in other words, the outperformance is concentrated in seats in BJP-ruled states.

In 2019, of the 59 close contests, the BJP won 41 and lost 18. It should have won half of 59 or rounding up 30 seats. But it won 41. Eleven seats extra and with a significant statistical deviation from 30 seats. This, Das claims, as evidence of modern-day 'ballot stuffing'.

Das goes on to admit that loss of 11 seats, if BJP 'intervention' had not taken place, would not have changed the election result. The BJP won 30 extra seats than required to win a majority, hence a loss of all 11 seats would not have changed the result at all. But the statistical result which needs to be honoured above all else seems to be the narrative-induced claim. Not very different from the result we saw in the discussion of V-DEM democracy rankings in contrast to the World Bank (WGI) and FH. V-DEM reached the bold conclusion of democratic sliding in India, based on subjective rankings; based on a combination of several subjective rankings, WGI authors did not concur.

But what did other statisticians say about Das's findings? Did they agree? They did not. Yajnavalkya was the first to question Das's results; Kapoor (2023) followed soon after. Interestingly, in the debate that ensued, *not one person defended Das's findings as 'accurate'*. The first point made by @Saiarav was that Das had *miscoded* the two centrally administered union territories (the Andaman and Nicobar Islands and Dadra and Nagar Haveli) – both of which the BJP lost narrowly – as non-BJP-ruled states and says, 'The basis for the classification is whether BJP has the alleged ability, due to its control of the local administrative machinery, to execute on electoral manipulation. The administration of the two aforementioned union territories come[s] directly under the Ministry of Home Affairs (MHA). Ergo, BJP has the same level of control over the administration of the two UTs as it has over the BJP-ruled states.'[6] The BJP's 59 close seats, it won 41 and lost 18, yielded a failure of the McCrary test (i.e. BJP manipulated the result). Correct coding would have yielded 51 close contests, BJP won 39 and lost 20. Further, 'This pattern of outperformance is not limited to NDA-ruled states. Out of the 41 seats it (BJP) won, nearly half are from non-NDA states,' Yajnavalkya (2023) added.

Das had contended, on the basis of his coding and data, that win losses in non-BJP states followed a random pattern and in BJP-ruled states it was not random and statistically in favour of the BJP. This simple correction now yields the @Saiarav result that in both BJP and non-BJP ruled states, there was a non-random result, i.e. both (or the whole class!) failed. Stated simply, all parties were gaming the system (ballot stuffing).

Building on Yajnavalkya's (2023) critique, Kapoor (2023) also undertakes a replication of Das's analysis, attributing the shortcomings to the interpretation of the statistical findings of the McCrary Test. Kapoor argues against the reliance on p-values (statistical probability value) to test the null hypothesis, emphasizing that positive results found in previous elections for both the BJP and the INC were incorrectly deemed insignificant due to the conventional threshold.

In 2009, for the INC, a positive result was found where it was more likely to win close elections; however, since it was classified as insignificant, it was assumed that there was no effect. In addition, Kapoor (2023) also makes a crucial point about the assumption that close elections are characterized by a candidate receiving 50% of the vote share; this need not be true in the case of efforts such as targeted campaigns towards specific groups of voters.

Close contests and the McCrary Test

There is near universal academic and political interest in the presence or absence of voting manipulation. As Bob Dylan might say, 'You don't need a statistician to tell you that'. The evidence presented in Das's paper is related to 'Close Elections', suggesting that the BJP won a *disproportionate* number of such contests. This key *assumption* behind the McCrary Test has been disputed by election experts working on black–white votes and results in US elections (Vogl 2011). Das forms his conclusion based on the 1977–2019 candidate-level general election results and the 2019–2021 state assembly election results. A natural extension of this would be to look at the universe of *all* the national and state elections in India for the two largest national parties – the INC and the BJP – and to put the BJP's performance in the 2019 general elections into a historical context. This is what we do.

Using the same specification as Das, with the winning margin of the BJP and the INC in close elections as our test indicator, we ran separate McCrary Tests for all the state assembly elections. Applying Das's method to the universe of all state elections since 1952 for the Congress and post-1980 for the BJP increases the sample size of the analysis to 369 state election years.

In *aam aadmi's* language, the larger sample allows us to place the 2019 general election in the historical context of all the elections that have taken place in India. We follow Das's lead and estimate the McCrary Test for each Vidhan Sabha election as a first cut of 'evidence' for potential voter 'manipulation'.

In layperson's terms, a p-value test is used to see if a null hypothesis or assumption is valid. The null hypothesis in our case is no voter manipulation. A rule of 'statistical' thumb for interpreting p-values is to see if randomness has a less than 5% chance of occurring (a p-value less than 0.05). If less than 5%, then the null hypothesis can be rejected. In our tests, non-random means a statistically correct likelihood of voter manipulation.

Figures 6.1 and 6.2 are examples of failure and success from the McCrary Test. Failure means non-randomness, and success (passing the McCrary Test) means randomness. Figure 6.1 shows the case where the McCrary Test fails using the BJP's 2019 winning margin in each constituency.

The difference between the solid black lines at 0 shows the treatment effect or the estimate of discontinuity whereas the dotted lines represent the range of estimates at 95% confidence interval. The running variable, which is the BJP's winning margin, is represented on the X-axis with either side of the cut-off point 0 being the constituencies that the BJP has won or lost. If the left- and right-hand bands do not overlap as in the case of Figure 6.1, we can conclude by looking at the graph that the result is a failure. Similarly, Figure 6.2 shows the case where the McCrary Test 'passes' using the INC's 2019 winning margin as a running variable.

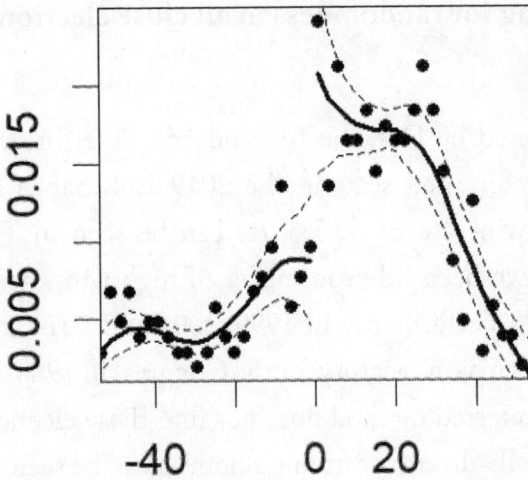

Figure 6.1: BJP's 2019 Lok Sabha Winning Margin
(McCrary Test)

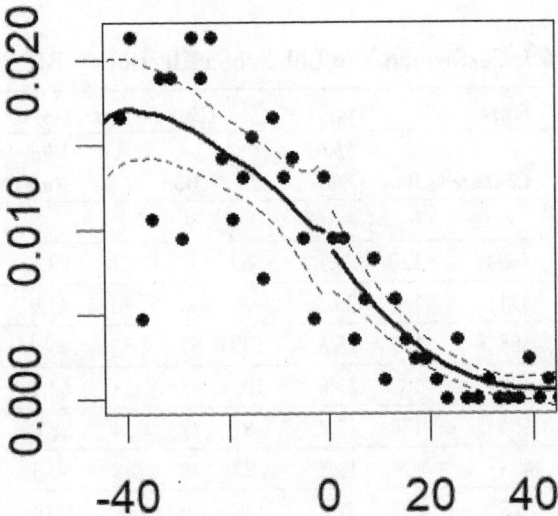

Figure 6.2: INC's 2019 Lok Sabha Winning Margin
(McCrary Test)

Looking for randomness in all close elections in India

As claimed by Das, the BJP indeed outperformed in the closely contested seats in the 2019 Lok Sabha elections with a win rate of 69.5%. As can be seen in Table 6.1, there have been other instances of high win rates such as the BJP's performance in 1999, 2004 and 2014, and Rajiv Gandhi's massive victory for the Congress in 1984; however, Das's preferred method does not find these elections to be statistically divergent from random as can be seen from the p-values. The BJP's win in the 1999 election in particular seems to have missed failing the test by a whisker with a p-value of 0.056!

Table 6.1: Performance in Lok Sabha Elections – BJP and INC

| Year | Seats | | Vote Share (%) | Close Contests (+-5) | | | | |
	Contested	Won		All	Won	Lost	Win Rate (%)	McP
BJP								
1991	468	120	20.1	69	37	32	53.6	0.849
1996	471	161	20.3	70	30	40	42.9	0.400
1998	388	182	25.6	109	51	58	46.8	0.125
1999	339	182	23.8	103	65	38	**63.1**	**0.056**
2004	364	138	22.2	81	47	34	58.0	0.130
2009	433	116	18.8	97	49	48	50.5	0.878
2014	428	282	31.0	48	29	19	60.4	0.687
2019	436	303	37.3	59	41	18	**69.5**	**0.007**

Year	Seats Contested	Won	Vote Share (%)	Close Contests (+-5) All	Won	Lost	Win Rate (%)	McP
Congress								
1962	488	361	44.7	101	53	48	52.5	0.815
1967	516	283	40.8	106	53	53	50.0	0.867
1971	441	352	43.7	47	19	28	40.4	0.106
1977	492	154	34.5	45	24	21	53.3	0.462
1980	492	353	42.7	77	42	35	54.5	0.852
1984	491	404	49.1	70	40	30	57.1	0.826
1989	510	197	39.5	100	52	48	52.0	0.834
1991	487	232	36.3	95	45	50	47.4	0.594
1996	529	140	28.8	109	51	58	46.8	0.983
1999	453	114	28.3	111	40	71	36.0	0.030
2004	417	145	26.5	90	34	56	37.8	0.064
2009	440	206	28.6	142	78	64	54.9	0.230
2014	464	44	19.3	54	20	34	37.0	0.171
2019	421	52	19.5	37	19	18	51.4	0.899

Sources: Election Commission of India; author's calculations
Note: McCrary Test p-value < 0.05 signifies potential 'evidence' of manipulation and a failure to reject the null hypothesis.

In Table 6.2, we present the top ten instances of outperformance in close contests as per the win rate in these contests for both the state assembly and the Lok Sabha general elections. The resulting 20 instances have a win rate exceeding the 69.5% obtained by the BJP in the 2019 Lok Sabha elections. In the assembly elections, we see that seven out of the ten instances of 'outlier' elections were won by the Congress by this measure. Congress's performance in Madhya Pradesh in 1995, Himachal Pradesh in 1985 and in united Andhra Pradesh in 2004 all resulted in failures of the McCrary Test (i.e. suggestive of manipulation). However, note that it is not necessary that the disproportionate win rate on its own would result in such a failure.

Table 6.2: Close Contests in Indian Elections

Year	Party	State	Close Contests (+-5)				
			All	Won	Lost	Win Rate (%)	Mc p-value3
State Assembly Elections							
1985	INC	Himachal Pradesh	12	9	3	75.0	0.04
1985	INC	Madhya Pradesh	63	45	18	71.4	0.00
1990	INC	Arunachal Pradesh	14	10	4	71.4	0.28
1995	BJP	Bihar	26	22	4	84.6	0.09
2002	INC	Uttarakhand	24	18	6	75.0	0.07
2004	INC	Andhra Pradesh	43	32	11	74.4	0.01
2006	INC	Tamil Nadu	17	12	5	70.6	0.24
2010	BJP	Bihar	22	16	6	72.7	0.82
2012	BJP	Himachal Pradesh	17	12	5	70.6	0.35
Lok Sabha General Elections							
1962	INC	Tamil Nadu	14	11	3	78.6	
1967	INC	Bihar	13	10	3	76.9	
1989	INC	Kerala	12	9	3	75.0	
1991	INC	Kerala	12	9	3	75.0	
1999	BJP	Bihar	11	9	2	81.8	
1999	BJP	Madhya Pradesh	12	10	2	83.3	
2004	BJP	Karnataka	11	9	2	81.8	

			Close Contests (+-5)				
Year	Party	State	All	Won	Lost	Win Rate (%)	Mc p-value3
2004	BJP	Maharashtra	11	8	3	72.7	
2009	BJP	Karnataka	14	10	4	71.4	
2019	BJP	Uttar Pradesh	16	14	2	87.5	

Sources: Election Commission of India; author's calculations.

Notes:

(1) States are chosen where there are at least 10 or more closely contested seats with a win rate among close contests of greater than 69.5% obtained by the BJP in 2019 Lok Sabha elections.

(2) Number of seats refer to assembly constituencies in assembly elections and parliamentary constituencies in Lok Sabha elections.

(3) Mc-p-value refers to p-value obtained from the McCrary Test resulting in failure of the Test or otherwise.

(4) McCrary Test results for Lok Sabha elections are not reported due to small sample sizes at the state level.

We then narrow the results obtained from our analysis to only identify instances where the McCrary Test fails, i.e. p-value is less than 0.05. In Figure 6.3, we present the instances where there have been such historical failures as measured by the p-value of the McCrary Test. A common theme in this select sample is a 'wave election'. In such elections, significant and widespread shift in voter preferences can and do occur towards one political party or ideology. The McCrary Test fails, a failure more likely because of wave characteristics than voter manipulation. Hence, interpretation of the results have to be more nuanced than 'yes or no'. Further, wave elections often coincide with increased voter turnout, as heightened political enthusiasm

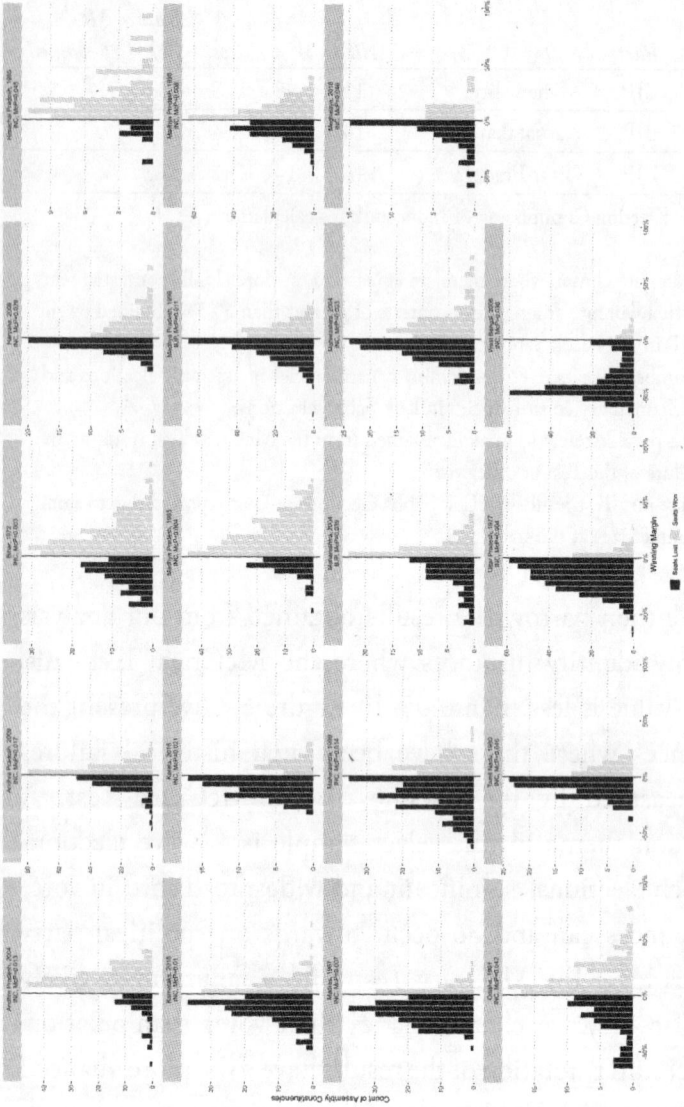

Figure 6.3: Disproportionate Wins/Losses among Close Contests in Assembly Elections, 1961–2023 Indicated as per McCrary Test p-values (Mc-P)

and engagement drive more people to the polls. The higher turnout can dilute the effects of any localized manipulation or irregularities, making it harder for the McCrary Test to identify discontinuities in the density of votes around thresholds.

Beyond the fancy statistical tests, each of which is built upon a set of assumptions, eyeballing the 2019 Lok Sabha results by close and non-close contests for each state is revealing. We have mentioned above that a key assumption behind the McCrary Test is the 'as-if random' nature of close contests. Then what about non-close contests? Would an incumbent party's incentives to campaign be reduced in a scenario where the ruling party is able to either precisely target the close contests or outright manipulate as claimed by Das? In Table 6.3, we present the results of the test 2019 Lok Sabha elections by close and non-close contests and the number of seats won in each of the categories.

Table 6.3: BJP – Close and Non-Close Contests in 2019 Lok Sabha Elections

State	Total Seats	Close Contests		Non-Close Contests	
		Total (%)	Won (%)	Total (%)	Won (%)
Andhra Pradesh	25	0	0	24	0
Assam	14	2	1	8	8
Bihar	40	1	1	16	16
Chhattisgarh	11	4	2	7	7
Gujarat	26	0	0	26	26
Haryana	10	1	1	9	9

State	Total Seats	Close Contests		Non-Close Contests	
		Total (%)	Won (%)	Total (%)	Won (%)
Jharkhand	14	3	3	10	8
Karnataka	28	4	4	23	21
Kerala	20	0	0	15	0
Madhya Pradesh	29	1	0	28	28
Maharashtra	48	2	1	23	22
Odisha	21	10	6	11	2
Punjab	13	1	1	2	1
Rajasthan	25	0	0	24	24
Tamil Nadu	39	0	0	5	0
Telangana	17	0	0	17	4
Uttar Pradesh	80	16	14	62	48
West Bengal	42	10	6	32	12

Source: Election Commission of India; author's calculations
Notes: A close contest is defined on the basis of a winning margin of 5 percentage points or less in the constituency.

Further investigations: what happened in Gujarat elections

In scrutinizing the historical instances where the McCrary Test falls short, an intriguing exploration lies in identifying where it succeeds, particularly concerning the much discussed 'Modi–Shah' model of election winnings. Here, the reference is to the present home minister, Amit Shah, a long-trusted confidant of Prime Minister Narendra Modi. A compelling avenue to evaluate Das's findings is to delve into the state of Gujarat, a stronghold where Modi secured victory in three consecutive state elections and served as the chief minister for an impressive 12-year span from 2002 to 2014.

In trying to examine voter manipulation, if any, by the BJP and/or the formidable 'Modi–Shah' duo in Gujarat, the examination unveils striking observations. In Table 6.4, rather than focusing solely on the disproportionate winning percentage in closely contested seats, our attention is drawn to the actual number of these close contests.

Table 6.4: Performance in Gujarat Assembly Elections – BJP

Year	Vote Share (%)	Seats		Close Contests (+-5)			
		Contested	Won	All	Won	Lost	McP
1980	14.0	127	9	3	0	3	0.203
1985	15.0	124	11	10	3	7	0.378
1990	26.7	143	67	22	15	7	0.068
1995	42.5	182	121	33	18	15	0.728
1998	44.8	182	117	29	14	15	0.624
2002	**49.9**	182	127	**50**	28	22	**0.950**
2007	**48.9**	182	116	**49**	23	26	**0.937**
2012	**47.9**	182	115	**50**	22	28	**0.164**
2017	49.1	182	99	57	25	32	0.714
2022	52.5	182	156	27	12	15	0.300

Sources: Election Commission of India; author's calculations
Note: In bold are the elections in which Modi was directly involved, either as a 'karyakarta' or chief ministerial candidate.

For instance, in 2002, the BJP contested 182 seats, winning 127 seats. What stands out is not just the disproportionate winning percentage but the fact that 50 of these seats were closely contested, underscoring the fervour and intensity of electoral battles. This trend extends beyond 2002, with subsequent years, such as 2007 and 2012, witnessing a consistent and noteworthy number of closely contested seats – 49 and 50, respectively (out of an assembly size of 182 seats). And in none of these close elections does the McCrary Test fail, i.e. there is no voter manipulation in states and elections where one would have expected the Das hypothesis to work best.

The distribution of the BJP's winning margins in the Gujarat state assembly elections are presented in Figure 6.4. Each bin in the histogram represents a 5 percentage point victory margin. Bins on the right-hand side of the cut-off point 0 represent the victories whereas the bins on the left are the losses. A failure in the McCrary Test means disproportionate wins or losses at the cut-off point, i.e. *the first bar on either side of 0*. Eyeballing the histogram explains why the McCrary statistical test does not fail for these contests – the BJP's wins among close contests are not statistically significant!

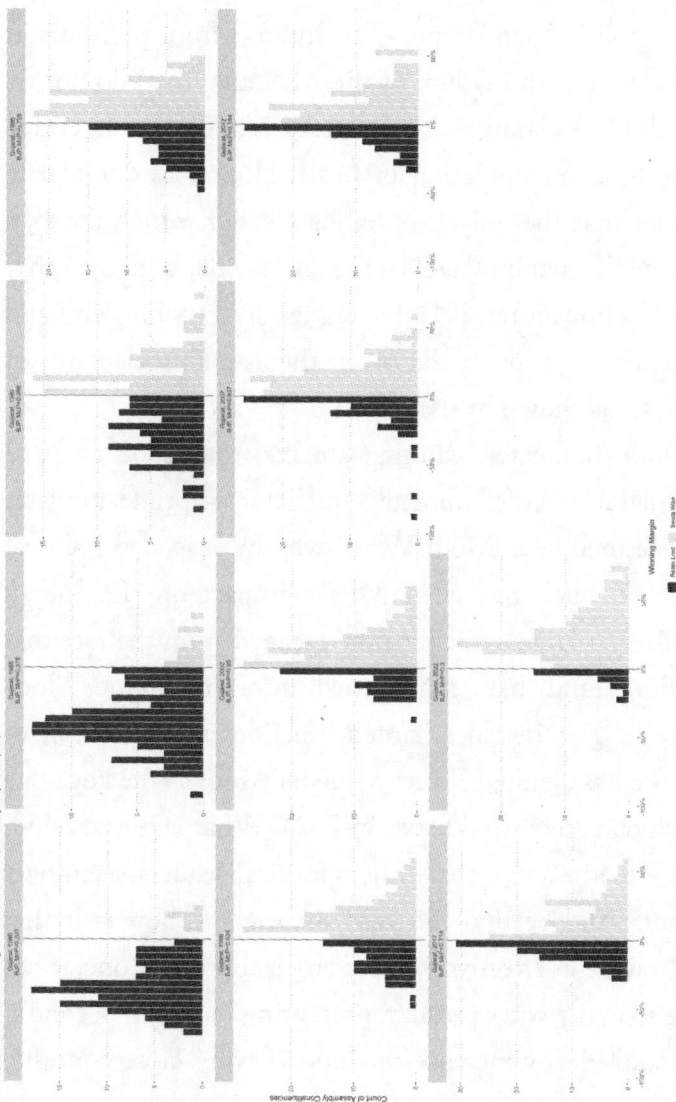

Figure 6.4: McCrary Test Results for BJP in Gujarat State Assembly Elections 2002, 2007 and 2012 Disproportionate Wins/Losses among Close Contests Indicated as per McCrary Test p-values

This surge in closely contested seats during the 'Modi–Shah' election years in Gujarat signifies a distinctive shift in the political landscape. Our findings from the Gujarat state elections (no failure of the McCrary Test) do not tie in with Das's claims that democracy is in grave danger due to electoral manipulation in India. How does one square the fact that the only Lok Sabha election which the BJP supposedly manipulated is the 2019 one, and no other state elections after 2019 (as argued by Das himself) and no evidence of manipulation in the assembly elections of Gujarat (as shown by us)?

Modi's unbeaten winning streaks from 2002 to 2012 in Gujarat as chief minister and later as prime minister were termed as a 'Modi Wave' even by seasoned political watchers. Such has been Modi's impact on the Indian populace at large, which can be gleaned from the fact that 'Modi's brand' has transformed into the 'Brand Modi' moniker. For instance, noted election analyst Prashant Kishore has claimed Prime Minister Modi as the key issue on which voters would vote in 2024. What is it that Modi brings to the table that other political leaders seemingly cannot? And beyond the vote share gains, how is it that any 'wave' can effectively affect an election? For one, it has to be spatially widespread, representing its reach. Secondly, it should ideally increase the 'floor' (swing close contests) instead of the ceiling (win easy seats by bigger margins) for it to translate into seats won. The BJP's performance in the

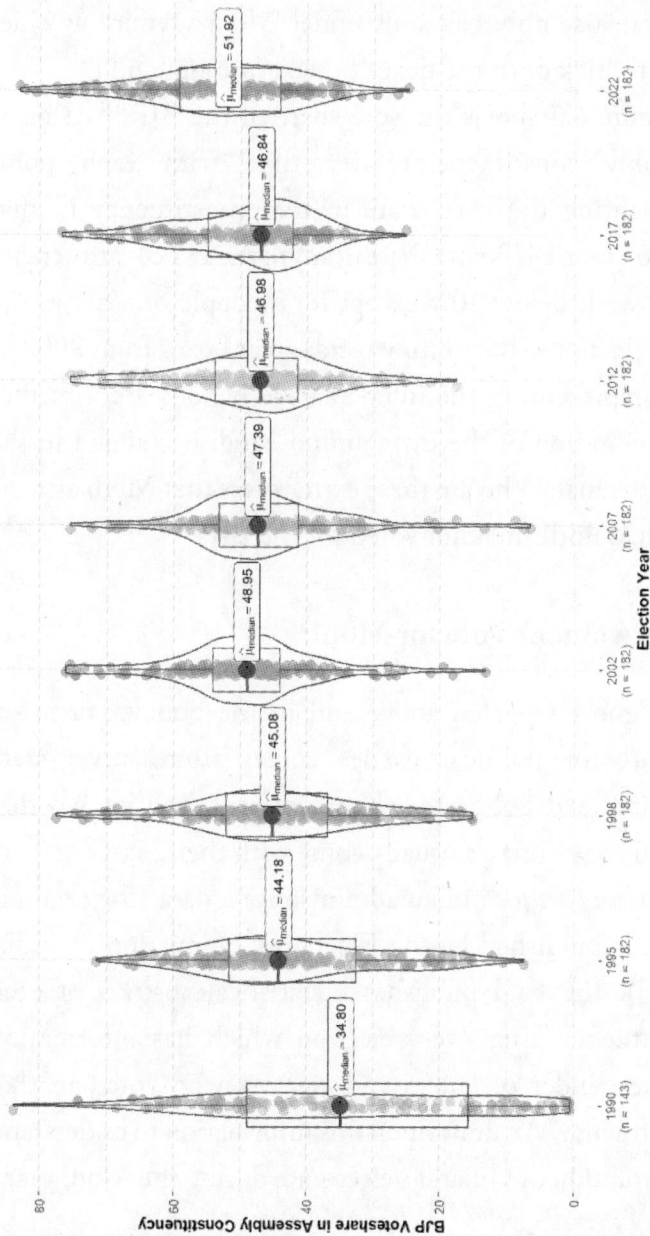

Figures 6.5: Evolution of BJP Vote Share in Gujarat Assembly Constituencies

Gujarat assembly elections under Modi's tenure as chief minister tick both the boxes as seen in Figure 6.5.

Figure 6.5 shows the vote share of the BJP in Gujarat assembly constituencies over time with each point representing the vote share in that constituency in that election year. BJP's vote share in any of the 182 constituencies never went below 10% except for a couple of seats in the 2007 elections. The narrow rectangular boxes from 2002 to 2012 representing the inter-quartile regions are a further demonstration of the extra ammo Modi has added to the BJP's arsenal. Who are these extra voters that Modi attracts who had until then not voted for the BJP?

Extra women's vote for Modi?

The figures reported above and in the popular press on support for political parties comes from survey data (opinion, exit polls, etc.). However, it is well known that the survey estimates usually come with their biases and are not *ground truths* unlike administrative data (for example the data published by the Election Commission of India, [ECI]). The ECI publishes a statistical abstract of each constituency after every election which has information on the gender of voters and electors who voted in that constituency. We draw upon this information to understand the evolution of Gujarat's electorate during the Modi years.

Table 6.5: Voting Patterns in Gujarat Assembly Elections, 1980–2022

Year	Electors Men	Women	Voters Men	Women	Turnout Men	Women	Gap
	(million)		(million)		(%)		
1980	8.3	8.2	4.5	3.5	53.5	43.2	-10.3
1985	9.8	9.5	5.2	4.2	53.2	44.4	-8.8
1990	12.8	12.0	7.3	5.6	57.2	46.9	-10.3
1995	14.9	14.1	10.0	8.7	66.9	61.8	-5.1
1998	14.8	14.0	9.4	7.7	63.3	55.0	-8.3
2002	17.1	16.2	11.1	9.4	64.9	57.9	**-7.0**
2007	18.9	17.7	11.8	10.1	62.3	57.0	**-5.3**
2012	20.0	18.1	14.6	12.6	72.9	69.5	**-3.4**
2017	22.7	20.9	16.0	13.8	70.5	66.1	**-4.4**
2022	25.4	23.8	16.9	14.7	66.7	61.7	-5.0

Source: ECI Statistical Abstract; author's calculations
Notes: The gender gap in turnout (female–male turnout) during Modi's years as chief minister are highlighted in bold.

From Table 6.5, we see that the heartbeat of the BJP's rise, consolidation and subsequent dominance in Gujarat resonates in the notable trajectory of women's vote share. From 1998 to 2012, there is a remarkable increase of about 5 million women *voters*, surpassing the growth in the female *electorate* during the same period, which stood at 4.1 million. This surge underscores the BJP's adeptness in cultivating and mobilizing women voters, hitherto excluded from political process, a demographic that has played a pivotal role in the party's political landscape. A significant watershed moment occurred in the 2012 elections, marking the zenith of women's suffrage during the Modi reign as the state's chief minister. The gender gap in turnout between women and men narrowed to a mere 3.4 percentage points, a remarkable feat in the political history of Gujarat. This reduction in the disparity between female and male turnout is especially noteworthy when juxtaposed against earlier years, such as 1995 and 2002, signalling a sustained and strategic effort by the BJP to enhance women's political participation.

The confluence of heightened female voter turnout and the surge in closely contested seats underscores not only the statistical trends but also the underlying narrative of political evolution and inclusivity in Gujarat. The BJP's ability to not only acknowledge but actively harness the power of women and grab that vote share has been a key driver in reshaping the political contours of the state and, later, the nation.

7

Giving Birth to Economic Narratives

The underpinning of this book, the reason it exists, is that it juxtaposes reality as we have always known it (namely official data) with the claims of those who disagree. Disagreements will always be there, something that is an essential part of (re)search and discovery.

What is different today as compared to yesterday? What is different today is that the differences seem unbridgeable – indeed, are chalk and cheese. Yesterday, differences were all on different varieties of only *one* kind of cheese. A concrete example is given by the divergence in opinion, data and 'facts' as provided by the private sector CMIE on female labour force participation rate, FLFPR, and that provided by the official statistical agency, the National Statistical Office (NSO). The private sector organization says FLFPR is less than 9%; the NSO says FLFPR is in the mid-30s. The official is four times the private; there is no meaningful way that the two are comparable. Why is the FLFPR important? Because it is a lens on issues important to the economy. It is a commentary on jobs (women not in the labour market because of lack of jobs); a commentary on gender equity (the whole world is watching, transforming, yet India is far behind) and economic growth (GDP is lower than officially proclaimed because there are not enough jobs, hence labour input is low, and output is low).

In the good old days, the debate would be of a few percentage points and would be as follows – the FLFPR in India is lower than it should be but with education it will get to where it should be. Differences in estimates of just 1 or 2 percentage points (you think the FLFPR is 24%; I think it is closer to 26%) and we would all go home marginally the wiser. Today we claim polarization and politicization and don't meet. And no question of meeting halfway, because that is giving equal credibility to both estimates (9 and 36) when one of them is most certain to be patently wrong.

Why is all this happening and how did it all start? It started with the government-supplied data on the Consumer Expenditure Survey (CES) 2017–18 being so off credibility that it opened the floodgates for questioning any and all data that the government published. Curiously, it has led to non-questioning of private sector data! There is a link there – the ecosystem.

Comfort and agreement with the familiar

For most of the period 1947 to 2013, India was ruled by just one political party – the Congress. As is natural, such monopoly brings in inefficiencies, corruption and a static mindset, a structure that both enables and encourages conformity.

The election of the BJP, led by Modi in 2014, upset the status quo for most players. However, the administrative bureaucracy stayed the same by definition. It is the same situation in the rest of the world – the rulers change, not the administrators. When there is a structural change in the rulers, well, the going gets difficult for all – and it may be especially hard for those who had thrown in their lot with the old regime of 'traditional' rulers.

The previous three chapters discussed the narrative (and reality) of democracy in India and what we understand about the fairness of elections. The next few chapters are concerned with improvements in the lives of the people and the economy – the two pillars of governance and outcomes of the quality of political and economic leadership. Both bread and butter are important, especially for the bottom half or bottom third of the population.

A strong 'capsule summary' indicator of improvement in welfare is the growth in per capita GDP. We had alluded to its importance in Chapter 2, and a very crude test we used there (attempting to predict election results by growth in per capita income) showed that there was a reasonably strong correlation between growth and election outcomes.

Economic growth (and its main engine, investment) is only one of the economic narratives that we will examine in some detail. But likely the most important one. The other three variables we need to look at are poverty decline, employment and unemployment, and taxation and redistribution. Note that the discussion on inflation, and its impact on votes, is conspicuous by its absence[1] for reasons I've mentioned earlier. As Monty Python might say, that is a dead parrot!

If in doubt, manufacture the evidence for the narrative

Emotions and narratives also run very high when the discussion concerns growth (and poverty). Why? India has been on a path of reform-led growth for the last 30 years, and voters tend to applaud and reward a good development performance. What is a poor 'Opposition' to do? Question the evidence put out by the government. And applaud all data that goes against the government, even if it is counter to all known evidence. And if counter data are not available, manufacture some (e.g. India needs 200 million jobs over the next 10 years).

There are other assumptions involved in the 'portrayal of a narrative'. For this a counterfactual helps – the recall of a time when things were better, coincidentally a time when the present target of disapproval was not present, and a system meeting with approval was. Recall the happier days. Notice the flurry of output stating that growth provided by the Congress was higher and better. The Congress is at a particularly low point in its evolution; a resurrection is possible by showing that the Congress led UPA provided a strong growth performance during the first seven years of its ten-year reign, 2004–13. And show it to be higher than a period of Modi-led governance which included the greatest shock (called Covid) the world has known since World War II.

However, as one compares the 2004–13 period in detail with the Modi record, it becomes more and more obvious that over a wide range of economic parameters, the Modi period was much better than the previous best period ever, 2004–13. Stated plainly but differently, the Modi period is the best ever on measurable economic parameters. This is not a wild assertion or exaggeration – we will provide facts documenting this 'excess' performance. And, we believe that the compelling nature of this excess performance has led the Opposition, collectively and individually, to *unrealistically* question the record and cast doubt on the reality. As mentioned in Chapter 1, this is what we may define to be the 'narrative'.

Narrative – question the data

One way any government's record may be called into question is via the questioning of official data. Almost as a side effect of governance, tax collection, administration of the justice system, etc., governments have access to a wide range of deep data that is unavailable to any other entity. Moreover, governments have an ability to aggregate and assess data, which simply cannot be matched by any private organization. But this also means that it is often hard to critique key official data releases. Hence, government data are an easy target. It is. The question remains – why did this not happen prior to 2014?

There are invariably error factors that arise when data is collated at scale even when the methodology is sound and calculations are made apolitically and in good faith. These errors are likely to be small (law of large numbers and all that). It is argued that in under-indexed Third World economies, GDP may often be understated since a lot of economically productive informal activity is not captured in the official data collection but it shows up in things like increased electricity usage. Studies linking power consumption to GDP data indicate that the latter can be unreliable. It gets even trickier where 'real' growth (nominal growth adjusted for inflation) is assessed since inflation calculations often involve complex methodologies and assumptions.

However, one of the central points in this book is that the world has changed radically. Computing power, big data, research into how to effectively handle the gaps, etc. has now progressed to a point where good researchers can pinpoint inconsistencies and holes in government data.

Government statistical systems are overseen by experts from international agencies. So while it can happen, it has become more difficult for either side, government or Opposition, to make legitimate objections. But that does not mean that whatever the government produces would be correct.

Our concern, as researchers and civil society, is to provide checks and balances to both the government *and* the Opposition. 'Plague on both houses' should be the guiding principle. So what is the answer to Lenin's query 'What is to be done'? Question both sides, weigh the evidence on both sides and decide which evidence is closest to the unknown truth. The reader can judge for herself. I critique several scholars, many of whom I know well. I want to be fair to them, fair to the government and fair to myself.

Quite apart from all this, do governments 'fudge' data in order to further political narratives? After all, it is usually in the rulers' interest to show high GDP growth and low inflation, for instance. Or that fiscal deficit is higher than stated. This happens, and has been happening for generations, and decades, and across countries.

Greece, for instance, triggered a financial crisis by making up its GDP numbers, and there's compelling evidence that the Soviet Union often indulged in similar falsification. The former Chinese premier, the late Li Keqiang, designed an index using three publicly available high-frequency indicators (electricity consumption, railway freight movements and bank credit) to act as a proxy for China's unreliable GDP data. Something similar has been done by a former Indian government economist, Arvind Subramaniam, and we critique his work, and judgement next.

GDP growth is over-stated in India – the first narrative

Many sophisticated tools are used to try and judge if official GDP data is unreliable, that is, outside the bounds of normal error. This is absolutely necessary. All data (government and private) contain errors. The question is – are such errors outside of normal? And if outside, are they due to manipulation? It is always in the interests of the Opposition to suggest this narrative and in the interests of the government to say all data and policies are correct. Hence, the responsibility on 'civil society' is enormous, especially in this fake information and fake commentary world.

This narrative path was initiated by none other than Mr Modi's own (former) chief economic adviser, Arvind Subramaniam (hereafter Subramaniam) in June 2019, almost simultaneously with the announcement of the election results for 2019. In a provocative piece (not unlike Das's attempt at calling out electoral manipulation as discussed in Chapter 6), Subramaniam alleged that India's

GDP growth was being overstated, and overstated by a gross margin.

GDP data around the world undergo revisions, so the exactitude of the revision is irrelevant; the alleged magnitude of overstatement is relevant, and is the story. By GDP overstatement, Subramaniam was claiming that the government had falsely estimated actual GDP growth to be near *double* that of official reality. His article was published within days of the news that Modi's BJP had won 303 seats in 2019.

Subramaniam brought all of his statistical acumen to 'confirm' that the gap between the actual and predicted GDP was as much as 2.5% and that this gap was statistically significant (i.e. it could not have happened by chance; in an eerie parallel to the McCrary Test offered recently by Das). Since Subramaniam believed that he had a model that could accurately proxy and forecast GDP growth, he thought he was broadly right in also *believing* the 'only' explanation for the gap between the official GDP growth and the predicted one is that the former, *and not the latter*, is in error. The official GDP growth is either fudged by the political masters or the error is due to the incompetence of statistical authorities around the world that vetted India's GDP measurement, or both.

Subramaniam's bold hypothesis rested on equally bold assumptions. Three assumptions were needed by Subramaniam to make his case.

Assumption 1: *Growth* in four real variables (exports, imports, credit and electricity) can adequately *proxy* real GDP growth for all non-oil-exporting countries with populations greater than 1 million.

Assumption 2: For all countries, the relationship cited in Assumption 1 is robust for two different time periods, in this case, Period I was 2001–11 and Period II was 2012–16.

Assumption 3: *Only India has a problem with official GDP data.* Hence, Subramaniam's entire analysis was geared to examine how much Indian GDP in Period II veered off from his predicted path.

If Subramaniam had bothered to test the predictions of his model for other countries, he would have found that for 46 countries there is no (statistical) difference between the growth of his predicted GDP and measured GDP as per the national accounts. The remaining 43 countries, were almost equally divided between statistical overestimation by national accounts by 1.7% and underestimation by an average of 1.8%. Parenthetically, see how Das's later work, in 2023, and on elections rather than economics, also claimed that the BJP had overachieved in closely held seats (i.e. overproclaimed its strength or achievements).

This equal division of model 'errors' should have been a hint to Subramaniam that the model was not producing much in the way of reliability. His concern was that India had overestimated its GDP growth. There are apparently at least 20 other such countries besides India. And which country does his model find is the worst offender, the one that is ostensibly cooking the books and/or whose statistical systems are most deficient? Germany! It tops Subramaniam's list – Germany has systematically overestimated GDP as predicted by Subramaniam by an average of 1.8% per year during the period 2012–16.

Like Das's political narrative four years later, Subramaniam's narrative of overestimated growth in India comes into question and falls under its own weight of inconsistencies. The legitimate question to ask is why is there a motivation to make a boldly inaccurate assessment and/or prediction?

Action follows reaction

Subramaniam's analysis was the first of the narratives casting doubt on Indian data (remember narrative is different from an academic and policy discussion about deficiencies in data and policy). Six months prior to Subramaniam's narrative, in December 2018, P.C. Mohanan had resigned as chief statistician of India. Why? Because the government decided to postpone the release of the first PLFS for 2017–18.

This is yet another area where government statistics often become contentious. A layperson might think that an individual is either employed (meaning earning something) or not. But there are many nuances.

For example, in a family-run business, such as a grocery store or a farm, the entire family may be stakeholders but the income may be officially clubbed as going to one individual. Then again, someone who is studying for a college degree or doing a PhD may not be looking for a job – hence not participating in the labour force. A woman who was employed may choose to get married and voluntarily take a break because her spouse has an adequate income – again ceasing to participate. Somebody who is employed but working outside the tax net – say a mechanic or plumber – may choose to conceal being employed or simply not be picked up by the data collection system.

There is also the quality of employment. A gig-worker delivering goods for Amazon might make more 'income' (meaning cash in hand) than an entry-level government employee. But most people would consider the latter to have more secure employment and better prospects. Moreover, different government departments can have different definitions and come up with different data. So there are many shades to employment, and since by definition employment or the lack of it is a political hot potato, there are many shades of opinion as well. What is critical, however, is that there shouldn't be many shades of fact.

The survey in question was the first NSSO (now PLFS) survey on employment and unemployment after 2011/2012 and hence the first authoritative NSSO employment survey post-Congress rule.

Such surveys have been conducted, at regular intervals, since 1983 and there wasn't a single occasion when a survey release was stopped. PLFS 2017–18 results were delayed ostensibly because the survey claimed an unemployment rate of 6.2%. As the headlines blared after the release (and after the June 2019 election), this was the highest unemployment rate in 43 years. In the period 2011–12, the unemployment rate was close to 2.5%.

The delay in the release of the data marked the first time in India's history when the results of household economic surveys were not released and/or not released on 'schedule'. However, it is true that the schedule has been elastic; in 2000, Arun Shourie, then the minister in-charge of the Ministry of Statistics and Programme Implementation (MOSPI), released the 1999–2000 CES before its scheduled time!

I was a member of the PM's Economic Advisory Council (PMEAC) in 2017–18, and had conducted a study, jointly with Tirtha Das, Professor IIM-Bangalore, for the PMEAC, which contained the following result: Two labour force surveys, conducted by the Labour Bureau (as different from the NSSO) for the periods 2013–14 and 2015–16, had reached the result that the unemployment rate in both years was close to 5%, i.e. much higher than the 2.5% reached during the period 2011–12.

It was common knowledge, among all people, that the economy dived in the last few years of the UPA regime. This was the inheritance of the BJP and Modi – an economy not in good shape, an economy that in 2013 was classified by all as a card-carrying member of the Fragile Five, an economy with a sharply rising unemployment rate!

It is doubtful whether the release of the employment report prior to the elections would have affected, as I am fond of saying, even the price of tomatoes. The delay just provided political ammunition.

But worse administrative action was to come. The all-important CES for 2017–18 was interdicted by the government. The report was never released, and neither was the ostensibly super-secret unit-level data ever made officially available.

As with any ban, this gave birth to a 'black market' (or cottage industry) in the release of selected portions of the banned report and speculative articles by those who had access to the data. It is anybody's guess why the government chose to stop the publication but of course, the political Opposition assumed the worst motives.

The interdiction also encouraged alternative survey agencies to gather their own data and profit from the enforced scarcity of official data. The administrative authorities did not realize, or appreciate, the fact that the banned CES data was needed for various policy actions, including the proper and efficient conduct of monetary policy.

What is even more tragic is that all the evidence suggests

that the government was absolutely correct in thinking that the CES survey was of terrible quality and, possibly, the lowest quality ever in the world, not just in India.[2] I remember writing that the government should release the data so that the world would be able to see the low quality of the work. Like the 1987–88 NSSO Employment Unemployment Survey, which produced bizarre estimates of total employment, etc. (the sampling weights were way off), the government can and should release all data, no matter how bad.

Release does not mean endorsement or acceptance

How bad was the quality of the data? None of the reporting and/or analysis and/or use of the leaked CES data (e.g. Jha 2019, S. Subramanian 2019, Ghatak-Murlidharan 2020) mention or discuss the quality of the banned CES survey. In other words, data has been accepted as correct.

Only one study (Bhalla-Bhasin-Virmani 2022) has questioned and/or documented evidence about the quality of CES 2017–18 data (Also see: Das, Thirthatanmoy, Bhalla, Surjit S., Bhasin, Karan and Motheram, Abhinav, 'Definition, Measurement, and Policy: Poverty Alleviation in India 1983–84 to 2021–22', Mimeo, 2024.). Without any exaggeration, I can confidently state that the quality of the banned 2017–18 data was indeed very bad, so bad as to make it possibly the worst quality household consumer survey published anywhere in the world, not just India.

I will provide several bits of evidence on the quality of the CES survey, and I am indeed surprised that no one, either within the government or outside, has bothered to do this analysis.

The government has set up committees to study the statistical operations and recommend changes. Most recently, in July 2023, the government reappointed a Standing Committee on Economic Statistics, which was first set up in late 2019, to restudy and reformulate answers to the same question: How bad is the quality of our official data on surveys, etc., and what can be done to improve their quality? To date, no public report is available of the committees' (2019 or 2023) deliberations. Nor do we know the nature of any corrective action or if any action has been taken. This is truly unfortunate since policy action depends on the reliability of data.

Our analysis of CES 2017–18 is based on publicly available data, either from the survey itself or administrative data or national accounts. It is important that this forensic exercise be patiently followed, because it goes to the heart of the narratives on the Indian economy.

First, this is the big picture as contained in CES 2017–18. Rural per capita growth between 2011–12 and 2017–18 (as per 2011–12 prices) was shown as -8.8% rural and 2.1% urban for an aggregate *decline* of approximately 5.5% over a six-year period. In our 75-year history, there have only been five declines in per capita consumption with the largest annual decline being 7.1% in the Covid year 2020–21. Except due to Covid, there has not been a single decline in consumption over the last 33 years. In 1991, per capita consumption declined by 1%.

What the NSSO reports is a decline of 5.5% over six years. An annual decline of 5.5% could be registered for 2017–18 only if there was *zero* growth in consumption in *all* the years between 2011–12 and 2016–17. Accounting for the real consumption growth as yielded by national accounts data, we estimate that the 2017–18 *annual* decline would have to be somewhere between 25% and 30%. Hence the conclusion of the 2017–18 CES data being the worst and most improbable ever. And a decline of such dimensions over a one- or two-year period would have led to widespread starvation or even famine across the countryside. And given its all-India nature, the worst catastrophe to befall India ever – worse than World War II, worse than the Bengal famine. *Yet, Indian scholars had no trouble accepting the CES 2017–18 results at face value.*

Other evidence about the quality of CES 2017–18

The Gini ccoefficient is a widely used measure of income inequality. A nation with absolutely equal incomes for all will have a Gini of 0, while a society where only one individual has an income and the rest do not would be at a Gini of 1.

India's rural inequality had stayed broadly in the narrow 1 Gini point range (30 to 31) since 1983. India's 2017–18 rural Gini was estimated to be 22.1, the *lowest ever observed in India and the world.*

The decline in rural Gini between 2011–12 and 2017–18, a change close to -9 Gini points, is off the charts India and worldwide. A change in inequality for two-thirds of the population (rural India) – a change almost three times the standard deviation for an average rural economy and more than five times India's own standard deviation for rural Gini – is unreal, and not possible. Again, the narrative intelligentsia accepted the data as 'truth'.

Such a significantly sharp decline in inequality is unheard of anywhere. The data by showing an absurdly large decline in growth and an equally absurdly large decline in inequality was sending red signals about its quality.

Let the reality sink in. The NSO collects data, tabulates it, analyses it and releases it for publication. Quality controls are normal and necessary, and the NSO (formerly NSSO) has been conducting surveys for 70 plus years. It was known to be a pioneer, at the frontier of household survey data collection and analysis. Then, after the non-release of data, committees were set up (though no reports even four years later are available). Experts have looked at the data and accepted it at face value, even though the government (correctly) found it fit to not stamp it with approval.

Table 7.1 presents data from various sources (national accounts, industry organizations, etc.) on items of consumption, food and non-food. Note that -5.5% is the CES 2017–18 comparator for all items of consumption, not just food. Meat, eggs, milk, fruits, vegetables and pulses – high elasticity food items averaged a per capita annual growth of over 5% in the period 2011–17. Electricity, cars, TV an airline passengers showed a per capita growth close to 7–8%, and medical and education a per capita annual expenditure growth of 7–8%.

It is a genuine mystery as to how the bad quality CES 2017–18 survey happened. It is an even greater mystery why otherwise vocal academics and social media and data experts have not commented on the bad quality of data. The story about narratives and politicization of all data produced by the government (especially growth, jobs, unemployment, poverty decline) is documented further in the next few chapters.

Table 7.1: Per Capita Growth Per Year of Real Consumption, Selected Items, 2011/12 to 2017/18

Item	2011–17 (%)
Food Items	
Rice	0.6
Wheat	0.4
Meat	5.1
Eggs	5.5
Milk	4.8
Fruits	3.5
Vegetables	3.3
Pulses	6.1

Item	2011–17 (%)
Non-Food Items	
Two-wheelers	5.8
Cars	3.9
TV	7.0
Fuel consumption	4.8
Electricity	5.6
Airline passengers	10.7
Railway passengers	-0.4
Mobile users	5.6
Social Consumption (National Accounts)	
Medical	8.3
Education	6.6

Sources: Various ministry annual reports, television data from BARC, automobile data from SIAM; as reported in Bhalla, Bhasin and Virmani (2022).

Once the government refused to release the CES report, it was 'open season' on its likely motives to do so. Many economists and statisticians have implicitly accepted that the report was not released because it showed the economy in a very bad light.

The Bhalla-Bhasin-Virmani study is the only paper (to date) to both conclude and substantiate that the data was bad and inaccurate – and that the economy was in good shape, at least much better than the CES claimed. Chapter 10 documents conclusions on poverty decline which is widely divergent from the CES 2017–18 data.

This detour helps explain some of the likely reasons why data narratives are the trend today in India and the likely reason why the Arvind Subramaniam paper on GDP growth was the first bullet in the reaction. Perhaps, a large part of the reason why Subramaniam's paper had currency and appeal was that the Indian government had created an environment compatible with the questioning of data.

Why did the government 'pioneer' the non-release of the public good called data. The delayed release and the ban likely reflected the insecurity and lack of confidence of some government officials who did not recognize the internal strength of the economy. Not unlike India preparing spinning tracks against England when they have three of the best fast bowlers in the world. (And the series had barely started when they met their comeuppance!) Analogously, the government started banning data when it did not reflect reality. Tragically, they were right about the data – we do find it to be the worst (in quality terms) consumption survey in the world and one which was in stark contrast to the underlying reality.

That is the real tragedy, for as we show throughout this book, Modi's ten years have provided the richest (all puns intended) development experience that India has ever experienced across a wide bandwidth of social and economic criteria.

8

Mother of All Narratives – Jobs and Unemployment and Wages

In this year of narratives with reference to elections, two prominent stories have been discussed and shown to be lacking in deep substance: GDP growth being overstated (circa 2019) and BJP votes being overstated in 2019 (circa 2023). The two stories are similar and parallel – GDP being overstated by the Modi government, and BJP votes 'fudged' by the Modi government.

We also discussed the reality about the NSO, a government organization, understating the consumption level in India in CES 2017–18 by a world record magnitude – and the economists and other experts *not* questioning the utterly bad CES 2017–18 data.

This chapter is a continuation of the same – how narratives are being played out via ideology, political preferences, polemics and polarization. All parts of civil society should be cognizant of this trend and the responsibility lies with them (that's us!) to call out the bluff and to identify all forms of fakery – fake news and its more subtle and, considerably more insidious, sister, fake commentary.

The grandmother of all data narratives is the one pertaining to jobs and wages in India. Job growth and unemployment are deservedly perennial political and economic issues, perhaps the most important economic subject for any society. (It is not exactly the flip side of economic growth, but close to it.)

If growth is present, can employment be far behind? And if there is job growth, can poverty decline not occur? And if economic conditions are improving, will the ruling party not be able to accumulate votes? These linkages are well known, and hence the concerted attack by the Opposition to make the case that what the official data is revealing is inaccurate and/or untrue.

All of us recognize this appeal, and as an economist whose major share of research continues to be poverty and employment, I strongly believe that employment should continue to be a major focus of research and policy. Jobs and unemployment are important concerns for any society, all societies.

The 'economic *narrative*' for India in the Modi election season is led by professors at leading Western universities and senior economic experts in India; their story is that much needed job growth is not happening, and if it is happening, then wages are stagnant.[1] Recently, Shashi Tharoor, both a leading intellectual and a leading member of the Congress party, opined that Modi has promised 20 million jobs a year and asked the rhetorical question as to from where these jobs will arrive. A good question, and as we will soon see, the workforce is not likely to exceed 7 million a year – and that is with an aggregate labour force participation rate (LFPR) of 60%. At 70% LFPR the jobs needed would be 8 million.

Narratives repeat themselves

Most electoral junkies will recall that leading up to the April–May 2019 election, an almost identical debate was taking place. In a paper prepared for the PM's Economic Advisory Council in late 2018, Tirtha Das and I looked at the debate regarding Modi's promises about generating employment. This is what we found:[2]

> It is popularly believed that *PM Narendra Modi had promised the generation of 10 million jobs a year. We find no record of any such statement.* In the BJP Election Manifesto 2014, there is the following statement 'The country has been dragged through 10 years of **Jobless Growth** by the Congress-led UPA Government'. At a campaign rally in Agra in August 2013, candidate Modi did talk about the lack of job generation in the UPA years. In the speech, Modi promised that if the BJP/NDA was to be elected, they would create 10 million jobs for the youth of the country ('youth' defined as those younger than 35 years). This is the only reference to job creation. There is no reference to the promise of 10 million jobs *per year* that we could find. [emphases added]

The coincidence with the present debate, allegations and promises not kept is staggering. This suggests that the cookie-cutter book on Opposition election campaigning has not changed over the last decade. Let us analyse how both the 10 million story and the 20 million story got to the press. There is a mention of 10 million jobs, though it is for the youth, and the likely time element of when the jobs will be created, was possibly three, if not five, years (the length of a parliamentary term). A reasonable interpretation of what the BJP election manifesto meant is 3 million jobs a year for the youth.

Which gets tripled in the narrative to 10 million jobs a year.

Wherefrom the allegation that Modi has promised 20 million jobs a year? Very likely this comes from Princeton professor Ashoka Mody's calculation (from *India Is Broken* and articles in the prestigious American media organization Project Syndicate). His estimate: 'India needs 200 million jobs over the next 10 years to employ its working-age population, and were starting from a decade that has experienced net zero or even net negative job growth.'[3] And there you have it – how Shashi Tharoor got his 20 million jobs a year. It was from Mody's preposterously wrong calculation (see below) that India needs 20 million jobs a year for the next ten years.

Jobs needed – UN population data settles the debate

The debate on jobs needed and jobs created has been a continuous discussion and debate point within India, and especially since Modi became PM in 2014. How does one settle the debate or the discussion, especially since private sector surveys on employment (e.g. CMIE-CPHS) are continuously showing lack of job growth in India between 2017 and 2022. And the FLFPR in India, again according to the CMIE, being the lowest in the world, ever! According to the CMIE, the FLFPR in 2022 was less than 10%.

There is a method by which some plausibility estimates can be constructed for assessing the various claims (e.g. Mody and CMIE) about jobs needed, and job growth, in India. The population and demographic experts at the UN present estimates of population by age and sex groups for most countries in the world and from 1951 to 2100. Census data are used when available.[4]

Figure 8.1 is useful in settling some arguments relating to job growth. The vertical axis represents the change in the *population* in the age group 15–64; this is represented by the dark line. The lower dashed line represents the change in the working age population that is expected to work and is drawn at a 60% labour force participation rate i.e. if 60% of the Indian workforce is expected to

be working, then this line represents the *new* jobs needed
per year.

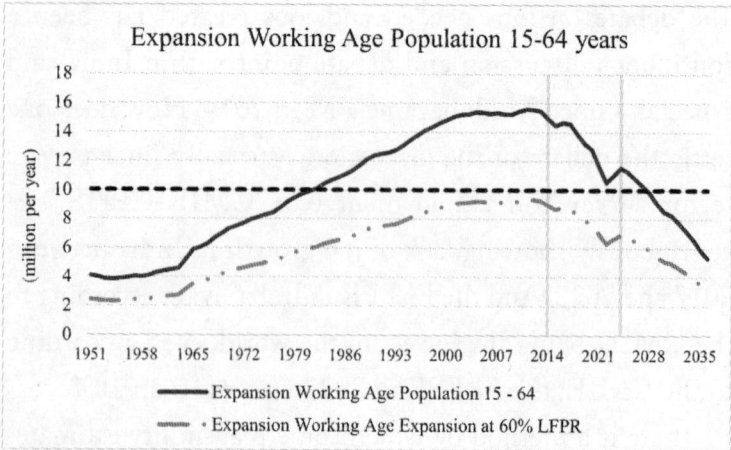

Figure 8.1: Working Age Population Changes

This chart puts into perspective the narrative nature of
'research' by Mody and others. Population decline is both
a global and Indian phenomenon. There is only one major
state in India, Bihar, where the fertility rate is above the
2.2 children per woman rate which keeps the population
constant (replacement level). Fertility declines have been
happening in India for the last 30-odd years, and we had
discussed in Chapter 2 how population growth in India is
now down to the 1% growth level a year, far below the 2 to
3% annual growth rate in the 1960s and 1970s.

These long-term population changes need to be
understood by those making job forecasts, over the next

few years. This chart is a ready reckoner for the potential number of jobs needed each year. The horizontal dashed line represents 10 million jobs a year. The dark line peaks at about 15 million increase per year in the working age group 15–64 years. This includes *everybody* in that age group – students, housewives, non-workers. *At no time in India's history has there been an increase in the working age population of 20 million a year. And at no time in India's history has job requirement,* ceteris paribus, *been more than 10 million a year!*

In 2024, total working population *increase* is expected to be 11.6 million; a 60% LFPR indicates that 7 million jobs will be needed to preserve the status quo on unemployment. An increase in jobs above 7 million will lower the unemployment rate, *ceteris paribus*; lower than 7 million will increase the unemployment rate. Population changes take place slowly, but the broad magnitudes of jobs required are correct for the medium term, e.g. five to ten years.

The broad population changes are very meaningful. Already, the population aged less than 15 peaked at 384 million in 2008–11. In 2024, this level is 32 million *lower* as a consequence of fertility decline. There will be less need for school buildings and already schools are being merged. The population age group 15–24 peaked in the last few years at 254 million and is now gradually declining at about 2 million a year.

What Figure 8.1 convincingly illustrates is that the 10

million jobs a year requirement is way over the top and not grounded in reality. What is a meaningful statement is that India's job requirement, *with an expected increase in participation rates*, is likely to be between 6 million and 8 million a year, not 12 million or 20 million as argued by some leading economists/narrative experts.

Issues regarding the measurement of jobs and job growth

We will now ground ourselves further into the reality of job growth in India, as revealed by the NSSO/PLFS and CMIE. Labour force data in India has been collected on a systematic basis by the NSSO/PLFS since 1983, and the workforce is divided into three categories of workers – salaried workers (generally formal employment and counting those who receive a monthly salary for work done), self-employed (whose income for the month is asked via one question – what were your earnings last month?) and casual workers (those who are employed on a piece rate basis). If a person receives no salary or wage but works for the family, this person is classified as a family worker. This is a common occurrence (unpaid family worker) in the labour force surveys in developing countries.

The International Labour Organization (ILO) has a strict definition of jobs worldwide – the job has to be either for pay or profit. If the work leads to monetary income for the family (e.g. wife sitting and 'manning' the shop) then it is a job. And in emerging economies, unpaid family work can be, and is, important. Hence, the argument that family work is not a job per se is not a valid 'narrative'.

Is it reasonable to assert that unpaid work is not really a job? This is controversial since even a casual visit to a shop or a farm will have women (and men) working as family helpers. Just because the incomes are pooled, does not mean that the individuals pooling their income are not working. If two brothers manage a shop (or farm) together and pool their incomes, is it not work?

Remember, the official ILO definition of work is whether the work is for pay or profit. An unpaid family worker is working for the profit of the enterprise (family firm/farm) and hence their labour should be considered work.

Very recently, the ILO has begun reporting the percentage of unpaid jobs in a few economies. Over the last 20 years, this fraction (more exactly unpaid family workers as a ratio of total workers) has fluctuated around 14.5% in India, with a peak of 20.1% in 2004 and a trough of 11% in 2018/19. In 2022, this fraction was 14%. In contrast, in a high labour force participation economy like Vietnam in 2022, this fraction was a much higher 22%.[5]

In Table 8.1 we present data on employment levels and changes over the last 40-odd years for total jobs, paid jobs and unpaid family work jobs. The data in this table will allow us to determine the number of jobs created, a key

variable in the election cycle of any and all economies. For
the period 2017–22, a total of 13.6 million jobs per year
were created, exceeding the 10 million 'target' set by the
narrative ('Modi promised 10 million jobs a year').

Table 8.1: Job Creation in India, 1983–2022

	Total	Paid	Unpaid	CMIE
Overall		(million)		
1983	233.9	192.6	41.3	
1993	309.8	239.7	70.1	
1999	341.1	268.0	73.1	
2004	388.7	294.3	94.4	
2011	400.2	327.2	73.0	
2017	406.2	354.2	52.0	408.2
2018	412.7	362.6	50.1	402.5
2019	442.2	376.8	65.4	397.4
2020	455.0	381.8	73.2	389.3
2021	457.3	384.6	72.7	399.2
2022	474.2	393.2	81.0	404.0
Per Annum				
1983–99	6.5	4.6	1.9	
1999–2004	9.5	5.3	4.3	
2004–11	1.6	4.7	-3.1	
2011–17	1.0	4.5	-3.5	
2017–22	13.6	7.8	5.8	-0.8

Sources: NSSO/PLFS and CMIE surveys; Bhalla et al. (2024), 'Female Labor
Force Participation in India: Measurement in Times of Structural Change'
Note: Currently Weekly Status definition of work; people with unpaid jobs are
also known as unpaid family workers in the NSSO/PLFS surveys.

The next highest pace of job growth was during 1999–2004 BJP coalition headed by Vajpayee. In contrast, between 2004 and 2011 (the much-cited high-growth period), total jobs increased at a very slow pace. Job creation (paid and unpaid jobs) increased by only 11 million in seven years, from 2004 to 2011. In Bhalla-Das, we document that there was zero job growth between 2011/2012 and 2014/2015 (this is obtained from Labour Bureau surveys).[6] Hence, a rough conclusion is that during ten years of UPA rule, 2004 to 2013, total job growth barely exceeded 1 million a year.

When the recent 2022–23 data were released, showing a 17 million job creation in the year, the narrative shifted to 'but most of the increase was due to increase in the unpaid labour category'. It was asserted that job growth was 'elevated' because of the 'fact' that several of these jobs were family labour jobs, and hence not jobs in the true sense of the word.

Even after the exclusion of family jobs, strong job growth during the last decade (the Modi years) stays intact. Excluding the unpaid jobs, i.e. only paid jobs, growth averaged 7.8 million a year between 2017 and 2022. Note that both categories of job growth (paid and unpaid) are the highest observed in NSSO/PLFS surveys for the last 40 years. Also note that the so-called promise of 10 million jobs a year was adhered to by the Modi government.

Also reproduced in Table 8.1 is the number of jobs created according to CMIE-CPHS, a private sector organization that first started disseminating survey data on the labour market in 2014. According to CMIE data, the total jobs in the 2017–18 economy were 408.2 million, almost identical to the PLFS study; in 2022–23, CMIE yields a 404 million employment total, and PLFS shows a 474 million employment total. These two sources are therefore wildly divergent after being identical for the period 2017–18. Many scholars have questioned the authenticity or reliability of the CMIE data (e.g. see Dreze- Somanchi).[7]

Notwithstanding the complaints/analysis of CMIE data on employment, the authoritative *FT*, in its review of the Indian economy over the last ten Modi years, states, 'The jobless rate has barely budged during Modi's time in office and exceeded 10% in October for the first time since the pandemic, according to the Centre for Monitoring Indian Economy, which produces India's most-cited unemployment figures.'[8] Job growth and unemployment are related; the unemployment rate according to PLFS in 2022 was 4.4%, a decline from 7.5% in the period 2011–12.

Table 8.2 shows the history of unemployment in India, and the reality is widely divergent from CMIE and/or *FT*.

Table 8.2: Unemployment in India, Ages 15–64 (million)

Year	Female	Male	All
1983	3.2	3.6	3.5
1993	2.7	3.2	3.1
1999	3.2	4.0	3.8
2004	4.1	3.8	3.9
2011	3.8	3.2	3.3
2017	7.6	7.5	7.5
2018	7.4	7.6	7.6
2019	6.5	8.2	7.8
2020	6.0	7.2	6.9
2021	5.0	6.2	5.8
2022	4.2	4.5	4.4

Sources: NSSO/PLF Suveys; Bhalla et al. (2024), 'Female Labor Force
Participation in India: Measurement in Times of Structural Change'
Data from NSSO/PLFS Employment and Unemployment Surveys, 1983–2022,
for the current weekly status of employment.

Data are presented for the current weekly status of
employment in answer to the question: 'Did you work (for
pay or profit) for at least 1 hour over the preceding 7 days?'
The more expansive definition of employment in India,
and more suited to Indian conditions, is the definition
of work as per usual status, i.e. did you work for at least
30 days in the preceding year. The usual status yields an
unemployment rate of 1 percentage point less than that
reported in the table for weekly status. And, the usual status
definition is closer to the CMIE definition of whether one
is employed or not.

Regardless, we get the strong result that the CMIE unemployment rate, as cited by *FT*, is close to three times the official unemployment rate. CMIE-*FT* claim that the jobless rate has not budged in the last decade, i.e. unemployment has remained stable at around 10%. PLFS data suggest a steep and steady decline from the 7.5% level observed in 2017–18.

A brief final comment on the ecosystem: A leading China newsletter, *AlpineMacro*,[9] reading the same 'expert output' as others, sounded very pessimistic about India's growth prospects. 'India has long been experiencing jobless growth,' it said. Experts (and journalists) have a considerably greater responsibility than the rest. They cannot, and should not, have the luxury of peddling fake 'expert' commentary.

9

Gender Advances to the Top in India and the World

It was symbolic but nevertheless pointed – a Republic Day parade where all the contingents were led by women. The goal of gender equity is now universal and we have to thank globalization and the internet and mobile phones for this much delayed advancement. Today, no matter what development index is prepared, gender equity is considered most important. There is also healthy competition among countries (and their leaders) to gain bragging rights in achieving more on this front. In a very fundamental sense, gender equity may even be said to have displaced concerns about poverty from its pride of place among social concerns.

A prominent narrative regarding India is that there is considerable bias against women. This assessment is historically accurate. Second only to China, birth control (or girl control) took the form of foeticide – abortion of a girl child via sex-detection techniques. Before the availability of sex-detection technology, India had, for centuries, employed other methods to ensure that the presence of girls in society was limited. Only now have infant mortality rates for girls become lower than that of boys, something that is the norm in the entire world.

Nature ensures that there is a balance; the normal sex ratio (number of boys born to girls born) is around 105, i.e. 5% more boys are born. But boys also have a higher infant mortality rate, which redresses the birth imbalance. The higher nature's infant mortality rate for boys can imply that, according to nature, boys are the weaker sex! Hence, to have infant mortality rates higher for girls (as India unusually has had for decades) is indicative of deep and persistent discrimination.

Prime Minister Modi has played an important role in enhancing gender equality. In my essay in *Modi@20*, I examined his Independence Day speeches and it is a no-brainer: the reality is that from day one, he has been a champion of women's rights.

In his first Independence Day speech on 15 August 2014, Modi shocked the nation by openly talking about 'open defecation'. Defecation, and words related to it, are seldom mentioned in polite company. It has long been known to health officials, and women, that the lack of toilets encourages violence against women and is a health hazard to all. Many experts have commented on the fact that open defecation is very likely a major cause of stunting and wasting in Indian children. It is unfortunate that the elite of India prior to Modi did not appreciate the significance of improved sanitation for people's lives – most likely because it did not affect them other than via impolite conversation.

Modi's 2016 Independence Day speech contained a powerful transformative message: *'Beti bachao, beti padhao'* (Save the daughter, educate the daughter). Those four words were revolutionary and many of us (women and men) said right on. It is the linking of the two (saving the life of the daughter and educating the daughter) that is revolutionary. Generations of political leaders – from Mahatma Gandhi, Nehru, etc. – have emphasized education for all. The female foeticide (abortion of a girl child pre-birth) rate in India, till around 2004, was the second highest in the world, second only to the one-child policy in China. It is this practice that Modi was referring to when he said 'save the daughter'.

Forever (at least since 1960), it has been well known that education (human capital) was the surest necessary way to success. It is interesting to recall that when Gary Becker came up with his analysis of the role of human capital, the conventional wisdom was that education was a luxury good – the upper class indulged in it to feel sophisticated. I don't think that was ever the feeling in developing countries like India – we were too poor for more than a small minority to obtain education.

Now here was a prime minister saying that we should educate the daughter. Modi did not emphasize the education of boys, thinking, correctly, that that is not where policy or encouragement was needed. Modi's vision of gender equity is best echoed in his own words:[1]

If we ensure two things for our mothers and sisters, i.e. economic empowerment and empowerment against health problems and we educate them, you can take it as an assurance that if even a single woman is educated in the family, if she is strong physically and independent economically, she has power to pull the poorest of the poor family out of poverty and therefore *we are working with emphasis on empowerment of women, health of women, economic prosperity of women, physical empowerment of women in our fight against poverty.* [emphasis added]

We will now present data on gender equity in India. We take it for granted that all women appreciate and support the equality initiatives. And that such actions will likely improve the BJP's vote share among women. In Chapter 6, we had noted how there had been a large increase in female turnout from 2002 to 2012 in Gujarat, and how this was also a period when Modi recorded massive victories in state elections.

Next, some facts indicative of rapid strides towards gender equity in India. There are more women in college in India today than men. Oxford University reached, after more than a 1,000-year history just a few years back, the milestone of admitting more women than men in its undergraduate programmes. This is a real, genuine revolution, which will have consequent effects on welfare, wages and occupations in the future. The percentage of female pilots in India is the highest in the world at about 15%, versus a 3% world average. Women enrolment in STEM in India is something close to about 42%, whereas in the US, it's something close to 31%; this level of enrolment is among the highest in the world. Later in this chapter we discuss the rapid increase in the labour force participation of women.

Table 9.1: Years of Education in India, Ages 15–64 and 15–24

Year	Ages 15–64			Ages 15–24		
	Female	Male	All	Female	Male	All
1983	2.1	2.2	2.2	2.2	2.2	2.2
1993	2.8	5.0	3.9	4.0	5.9	5.0
1999	3.4	5.7	4.5	4.9	6.5	5.7
2004	4.3	6.6	5.5	6.2	7.5	6.8
2011	5.5	7.5	6.5	7.9	8.7	8.4
2017	6.4	8.2	7.3	9.2	9.6	9.4
2018	6.7	8.4	7.6	9.4	9.8	9.6
2019	6.8	8.5	7.6	9.6	9.8	9.7
2020	6.9	8.6	7.7	9.7	9.9	9.8
2021	7.0	8.7	7.9	9.8	9.9	9.9
2022	7.0	8.5	7.8	9.8	10.0	9.9

Source: Data from NSSO/PLFS surveys 1983 to 2022; Bhalla et al. (2024b), 'Female Labor Force Participation in India: Measurement in Times of Structural Change'.

Now to some specifics on gender transformation. Table 9.1 documents the level and speed of structural change. Too often, the discussion about gender equity in India looks at the education gap for the working population of 15–

64 years. In the 2004–05 period, the average educational attainment of the working population was just 5.5 years, and that of women was two-thirds of men (4.3 years for women vs 6.6 years for men). In 2022, there was still a considerable gap – 7 versus 8.5 years.

When a society is undergoing structural change, data on long-run averages is not very meaningful in areas of education and health. This is because of the legacy effect. For example, the 50-year-olds of today were born in the 1970s! Their lack of education will 'contaminate' all education averages from 1976 onwards.

Structural change means a rapid change across time. More meaningful therefore is to look at those who went to school recently or are going to school (the 15–24-year-olds). Interestingly, there was complete gender equality for 15–64-year-olds and for the youth in 1983. It is not clear how much of this is an indication of gender equality and how much was a measurement error. Very likely neither. Most likely an indication that only the elites were going to school and not others.

By around 2011, gender parity in education was achieved. And it is likely that we will soon see educational attainment among the 15–24-year-olds to be higher for women than men – the norm in upper-income and advanced countries.

Gender equity in the labour market

It is alleged that an important sign of gender inequity in India is the low rate of female labour force participation in India. But as with education, change is happening and happening fast. Table 9.2 documents the speed of this change. The first column documents the change in **labour force participation rate** (LFPR) for females (female **labour force participation rate or** FLFPR) according to the current weekly status or CWS of NSSO/PLFS (if you worked, did you work at least one hour last week?). The second column has the CMIE estimate of FLFPR. The third column has the NSSO/PLFS estimate for males and the fourth column the LFPR for all population.

First, note that there seems to be a break in the series in 2011/2012. It occurs for both males and females (though for women it is twice the decline) and is likely to do with some aspect of definitional change in the measurement, and structural change. Both aspects are explored in some detail in Bhalla et al. (2024).

More important is the trend from the 2011–12 period onwards. Note that the aggregate LFPR in 2022 is at its highest level since 2004. Not reported is the LFPR for the 'usual status' of employment. This level was a high 39.2% in the period 2022–23, rather than 33.2% as per the CWS. According to all definitions, the FLFPR is at its highest level today, post 2004. Further, at 61% LFPR for all workers (usual status), India's LFPR is finally becoming respectable again. However, there is no question that the LFPR needs to be closer to the 70 level, and no question in our mind that it is likely to get there by the early 2030s, if not sooner. (See Bhalla et al. 2024.)[2]

Table 9.2: LFPR in India, 1983–2022, 15–64 years

Year	PLFS Female (%)	CMIE Female (%)	PLFS Male (%)	PLFS All (%)
1983	32.9		86.0	60.1
1993	37.2		85.7	62.0
1999	35.5		84.5	60.6
2004	38.8		85.1	62.5
2011	28.4		81.1	55.3
2017	22.1	12.1	77.6	50.4
2018	22.6	11.5	77.9	50.7
2019	27.7	11.1	78.3	53.5
2020	28.9	9.9	77.9	53.9
2021	28.7	9.7	79.1	54.5
2022	33.2	9.3	80.7	57.1

Sources: NSSO/PLFS surveys 1983–2022; CMIE surveys 2017–18 to 2022–23.
Note: Bhalla et al. (2024), 'Female Labor Force Participation in India: Measurement in Times of Structural Change'.

Why is it news that Indian women are now working at the highest rate since 2004? For two reasons. First, the FLFPR is now at approximate South Asian levels, though still some distance away from where it should be.

Second, and most importantly, because the dreaded narrative word is applicable again. The source of the FLFPR narrative is CMIE. In the previous chapter we had documented that CMIE claimed that there had been a decline in employment since the 2017–18 period. On the FLFPR, their estimates are even more bizarre and happily lapped up by the usual suspects in the media and Opposition. Specifically, their estimate of the FLFPR for India at 9.3% is approximately one-fourth of the official PLFS estimate. Further, it is the lowest such estimate in the world and lower than Yemen and Iraq. Is that possible? And where from does a respected publication like *FT* get the following, which is neither fish nor foul: 'Women account for a smaller percentage of the labour force than when Modi took power in 2014. India's FLFPR fell from 25 per cent in 2014 to 24 per cent in 2022, lower than regional neighbours Bangladesh, Sri Lanka and Pakistan.'[3]

There is further good 'anti-narrative' news on the wage gap between men and women. Table 9.3 documents the wage gap for selected countries for both intermediate (less than college but greater than 10th standard) and advanced (greater than or equal to college) education. The wage gap for college-educated workers (circa 2022), 16.7%, is among the lowest in the world and lower than high-income economies where the average wage gap is 19.7%. India is close to Mexico, while Bangladesh, with 8.6%, seems to have the lowest wage gap among the countries selected.

There is further good news on gender equity in India. For all unmarried college degree workers, the wage gap is almost non-existent – only 3% in the 2022–23 period (for the US, it is 6%). No matter how you slice the wage data, the Indian record is one of consistent improvement over the years and of low wage gaps – for college-educated workers, the numbers are comparable and likely better than for several advanced countries.

Given these statistics, the legitimate question arises: from whence the narrative, and why does it have so much currency among only a few domestic and international scholars/journalists/people?

Table 9.3: Mean Gender Pay Gap by Educational Attainment (%)

Country	Intermediate	Advanced
Bangladesh	-2.5	8.6
Brazil	28.0	32.1
India	48.0	16.7
Indonesia	61.6	33.3
Mexico	18.2	15.8
Pakistan	41.1	35.2
Sri Lanka	20.1	34.4
Thailand	20.9	15.5

Country	Intermediate	Advanced
Country Classification		
High Income	25.3	19.3
Upper Middle Income	21.8	17.6
Lower Middle Income	18.3	16.0
Low Income	4.5	18.6

Source: Bhalla et al. (2024), 'Female Labor Force Participation in India: Measurement in Times of Structural Change'.
Note: Wage gap is (male wage–female wage)*100/male wage.

10

Elimination of Extreme Poverty in India – Will It Affect Choice 2024?

Progress on poverty has a large political dimension. If growth in GDP matters most for elections in advanced economies, poverty decline matters most in emerging economies. Hence, there is a need for a proper understanding of what has happened, is happening and is likely to happen to poverty in India.

As we discussed in Chapter 7, the household consumption survey for the 2017–18 period was not released by the government. As we were going to print, the government released some results from the CES 2022–23 survey. Fortunately (for this book), the released results are very close to the results contained in the 2022 *IMF Working Paper* (BBV) that has been cited. The results of the India Human Development Survey (IHDS) 2022–23, a private-sector survey conducted jointly by the University of Maryland and India's leading think tank, the National Council of Applied Economic Research (NCAER), have not been released.

The narrative – again

In the absence of official data, we can all come up with our own estimates. There is no benchmark and therefore no official 'truth' to verify. There are therefore narratives at play on this most important political and economic subject.

The first narrative, as contained in the conclusion of a recent 2023 article by two academics, Maitreesh Ghatak and Risabh Kumar, of prestigious foreign universities is as follows: 'As the 2024 elections approach, taking stock of the economy after a decade-long rule of the government led by Prime Minister Narendra Modi becomes a natural talking point.'[1] After a discussion of the political importance (with which we agree), the authors conclude: 'headcounts from a wide range of estimates puts India's poverty at between 20–25% prior to the pandemic.'

Ghatak and Kumar are not very precise about where they got this estimate and they admit it with the phrase 'from a wide range of estimates'. Our publishers won't allow us this luxury on an important political economy subject, especially in this election year! So pardon us as we get slightly technical and hopefully present all sides of the debate in a non-boring technical fashion.

Here we go. Headcount is the number of people below a specific consumption level, which is deemed to be the defined poverty line separating the poor from the non-poor. There are reams of theoretical and empirical literature stating that such a definition is fuzzy and that people around the line are the 'precariat', i.e. they have an insecure income and can be non-poor today and become poor tomorrow. As we will soon see, just getting hold of a headcount is hard enough; hence, we will confine ourselves to the narrower question of what happened to poverty in the last 20-odd years.

One more bit of technicality. Measurement. The easy part – we will define the poverty line in terms of consumption per person. And how do you measure consumption? By doing a survey of representative households, as the NSSO had been doing since 1951. In the survey, questions on a few hundred items of consumption are asked, with each question for the household estimate of how much rice, wheat, fruits, vegetables, shirts, shoes, electricity, motorcycles, refrigerators, cars, etc., was consumed over the last 30 days. Oh yes – even salt. (This last *uniform* 30 days purchase method is called the Uniform Recall Period [URP]).

But the world has changed since 1951. Hence the new method of estimating consumption is via a Modified Mixed Recall Period (MMRP). Jargon aside, the MMRP method allows for different memory recall periods for different items of consumption. For example, the recall period for perishables is 7 days, electricity is 30 days and consumer durables is 365 days. The logic is that if we bought a TV or ceiling fan or scooter (all consumer durables) in the last year, we're likely to recall the purchase. We're also likely to recall our last electricity bill. We're less likely to recall the quantity of potatoes we bought four weeks ago.

This is a significant improvement over URP, but don't tell that to those interested in narratives. Why? Because the MMRP results amount to 10% less headcount poverty rate for the same year and for an identical poverty line! For example, for the 2011–12 agricultural year, the official MMRP estimate is 12.2% poor; for the URP estimate, 21.8% poor. That is a difference of 9.6% of the population or 124 million. Let this first fact – this huge discrepancy – sink in. An improved definition of poverty (MMRP method) just led to 124 million people being defined as non-poor.

Now back to slightly less technical details of change in poverty. When Ghatak-Kumar state that poverty today is 20–25% (and before the pandemic) they either mean that poverty has gone up by 13 percentage points since the period 2011–12 (reminiscent of the results of the banned NSSO 2017–18 survey) or they mean that poverty has stayed approximately the same in the decade post 2011–12.

Let us be generous – assume that Ghatak-Kumar are using the old, discarded URP method of poverty measurement, the one that yields an artificially higher estimate of poverty (124 million more people poor as explained earlier – and poor by the obsolete URP definition). According to this generous interpretation, one is led to conclude that whatever improvement in real consumption (also called growth) that happened between 2011 and 2019 had zero effect on the consumption of the bottom fifth of the population. And that despite no change in their consumption for a decade, the poor still came out to vote for Modi in 2019. In the 2019 election, the Congress obtained 19.5% of the vote. So does the narrative amount to a claim that the Congress, whose slogan in 1971 was *Garibi Hatao*, got all the bottom 20% vote and no more?

There are more absurdities in the narrative. Over the last decade (2011–12 to 2021–22), per capita GDP in India increased by a cumulative 52%; real per capita consumption (national accounts data) increased by 37%. If you go by this paper, not a single paisa of this increase went into the pockets of the bottom 20% to 25%. Does that pass the smell test?

Estimates of poverty in India, 2004–2022

The lack of official release of the consumption poverty data does not mean we have to operate in semi-darkness. Researchers and policymakers will move on even if statistical departments passionately cling to their bans and delays (like in the non-release of the 2022–24 CES data to date).

Towards this end, two co-authors (Karan Bhasin and Arvind Virmani) and I attempted to track the level and change in Indian poverty since 2011–12. This was published as an IMF Working Paper in April 2022 (hereafter BBV 2022). Several conclusions were reached, with perhaps the most important (and therefore the most controversial) being that in the year of the pandemic, 2020–21, India had achieved one major goal. This was the elimination of extreme poverty defined by the consumption level of purchasing power parity (PPP) $1.9 per capita per day by the MMRP definition of poverty (or ₹1,415 per month per person in 2020–21 prices). Elimination here means that less than 1–2% of the population had consumption less than the poverty line.

(It would take us far afield to explain the concept of PPP, which is generally worked out by comparing the price of the same basket of goods in two nations, rather than using the official exchange rate. Suffice it to say that 1 PPP $ of consumption = approximately ₹23).

At first, the dean of poverty measurements – the World Bank – baulked at our results because we had formally incorporated government food subsidies into the estimate of the total consumption of those who received the food subsidy – the poor (actually the bottom 50% of the urban population, and the bottom 75% of the rural population as per the 2013 Food Security Act). After first questioning this, the World Bank agreed that in-kind food subsidies should be included in total consumption and therefore the measurement of poverty.

Over the years, the Modi government has provided

a considerable amount of support to the poor – besides free food (10 kg per person per month of free wheat or rice) it has expanded or introduced subsidies for LPG cylinders, housing, employment (the Mahatma Gandhi National Rural Employment Guarantee Act, or MNREGA), scholarships for education and fertilizers. Not all subsidies accrue to all. The data are available on the government Direct Benefit Transfer (DBT) website.[2] We exclude fertilizer subsidy because it is a production, not a consumption, subsidy. Consumption (DBT) subsidies in the period 2022–23 were approximately equal to ₹4.8 lakh crore or ₹4.8 trillion (1 trillion = 100,000 crores); private consumption was equal to ₹164 trillion, so such subsidies amounted to about 2.9% of total consumption.

Taking a conservative estimate that DBT subsidies accrue equally to all the 756 million receiving the Public Distribution System (PDS) subsidy, one arrives at a per person transfer of ₹529 per month. The average poverty line in the 2022–23 period was ₹1,726, so the subsidy amounted to about 31% of the World Bank PPP $1.9 poverty line or 18.2% of the PPP $3.2 poverty line (at ₹2,906 per month in the 2022–23 period).

These are large transfers and consequently have large effects on poverty reduction. Effectively, as we show in Table 10.1, extreme poverty has been eliminated in India (helped enormously by transfers amounting to 2.9% of total consumption or about 1.7% of GDP). These are effective

Table 10.1 : Poverty and Its Decline – 2004 to 2022, Various Methods and Sources

Country	2004	2011	2022	2004–11	2011–12
	Poverty Headcount (in % of population)			Poverty Headcount Change (in % of Annual change CAGR)	
World Bank PIP data, URP poverty line, PPP$ 3.2					
Bangladesh	65.8	60.0	43.0	-1.3	-3.0
China	43.2	23.5	1.0	-8.7	-28.7
Indonesia	57.3	41.9	15.8	-4.5	-8.9
India	76.3	61.7	45.9	-3.0	-3.0
Vietnam	59.3	13.0	5.0	-21.7	-8.7
India – BBV (2022) and update using DBT					
India MMRP – BBV (PPP $1.9)	31.9	10.8	0.9	-15.5	-35.5
India URP – BBV (PPP $3.2)	80.1	62.9	29.9	-3.5	-6.8
India MMRP – BBV method, update (2024); with food subsidies only	73.5	52.2	18.1	-4.9	-11.8
India MMRP – BBV method, update (2024); with food subsidies plus DBT	67.6	52.2	6.7	-3.7	-18.7

Sources: World Bank. (2023). Poverty and Inequality Platform (version 2017 PPPs: 20230919_2017). World Bank Group. www.pip.worldbank.org. Accessed 01 Feb, 2024; Bhalla–Bhasin-Virmani (2022); authors computations.

Notes:

1) Data are chosen for the year closest to 2004, 2011 and 2022. The World Bank final year data for India is 2021.

2) Rates of change may be approximate for countries other than India.

3) All computations done for the PPP $3.2 line, unless otherwise stated.

transfers given minimized leakage via fintech. In the period 2022–23, we find that post-transfers even for the higher PPP$ 3.2 poverty line, the level of poverty in India is less than 10%, and closer to 7%.

From the World Bank poverty data website[3] one can obtain a comparative poverty picture of the best-performing Asian economies. For the PPP $3.2 poverty line, the latest year estimates (between 2020 and 2022) are as follows: Bangladesh 43%, China 1% and Vietnam 5%. As we show in Table 10.1 the India estimate, with DBT subsidies excluding fertilizers, was a comparable 6.7%.

Table 10.1 contains comparative data for five countries – Bangladesh, China, Indonesia, India and Vietnam – as made available by the World Bank on its PIP (Poverty and Inequality Platform) website. Unit-level data for China is not made available to researchers outside the World Bank – we are only reporting it because China is an important country for all comparisons, especially poverty. The India data reported by the World Bank is for a synthetic estimate of poverty using CMIE-CPHS data with the unusual intervention by the World Bank authors (Roy and Weide) of changing perhaps the most sacrosanct variable in household surveys – the population weights. This was done to accommodate the serious criticism of respected scholars like Dréze that the CMIE-CPHS population weights were far removed from reality.

Two columns (labelled 2004 to 2011 and 2011 to 2022)

report the second primary variable of interest – the pace of (log) decline of the headcount PPP$ index of poverty.

There are two estimates available for poverty reduction in India for the period 2004–05 to 2021–22. Data as per DBT transfers and using the BBV methodology for the MMRP method, and that provided by the World Bank for the URP method (available at www.data.worldbank.org).

Note the huge difference in poverty estimates for India for 2021. The World Bank, using the obsolete URP method and CMIE data on consumption, arrives at a 45.9% estimate for the PPP $3.2 line. Bhalla-Bhasin-Virmani estimate (incorporation of just the food subsidy) 0.9% (PPP $1.9 line) and 18.1% (PPP $3.2 line) for 2020 (the last year of data in the 2022 IMF Working Paper). Incorporating DBT transfers, the poverty estimate for the PPP $3.2 line for India is markedly lower at 12.6% poor in 2020 and 6.7% poor in 2022, compared to 52.2% in 2011. The reader can choose her own time period of comparison (or contrast). The incorporation of DBT subsidies allows India to have the second-highest pace of poverty reduction between 2011 and 2022 *and at more than twice the pace for all countries excluding China.*

There are several questions we can ask of each set of data, but the most important, for this book about policies, politics and elections, is which government regime, UPA or BJP–Modi, had a greater effect on poverty levels and their decline. This assessment is likely being done by low-income voters who will ask themselves which government has benefited them more. The answer seems unambiguous, especially after the important correction for the pro-poor DBT subsidies provided by the government. The deep and fast reduction in poverty (at close to 20% per annum phase 2011 to 2022) makes it more likely that voters will vote for the incumbent BJP government in increasing numbers. And it will not be lost on the voter that compared to other nations they (and India) are doing better than at any time in history.

Marx is reputed to have said that if religion did not exist, he would have had to invent it. In India, if poverty did not exist, it would have been invented by Marx's comrades. There is, however, a transformation that has become apparent in all countries, rich and poor, advanced and developing. The concept of poverty has shifted from absolute to relative. This shift is most apparent in India today and it started becoming apparent in China five to ten years ago.

These results also have a message for our policymakers. Time to raise the poverty line *to at least the PPP $3.2 level* (₹1,726 per person per month in 2023 prices) and rethink the targeting of the poor – why not 50% of rural India and 25% of urban India as beneficiaries of DBT transfers? This also yields the World Bank historical bottom 40% of the population as the target for attention and delivery. This will also mean that each *poor* person will receive more, a boon to welfare and equality.

Learning poverty

As countries attempted to emerge out of colonialism or underdevelopment or both, two policies were considered essential – reform of agriculture (land reform) and expansion of education for the masses – and on both we failed in our early decades (50-plus years) of independence. On agriculture, we continue to fail. The 1991 reforms, transformative as they were, and necessary and pioneering and brilliant, sadly did not attempt to reform agriculture. Many of the elites (including myself) were major beneficiaries of the elite bias of our first prime minister Jawaharlal Nehru. We applauded the building of institutions like the IITs (rather than the expansion of primary education for all), and many of my colleagues and friends over the years still say this was a 'good' policy. Look at our software exports, they ask – would that have been possible without the early expansion of IIT-like temples of wisdom? Yes.

What differentiates India and China from the rest of the world is *size*. Today, Indian and Chinese populations are equal – at around 1,400 million. The next largest population resides in the US – there are around 330 million Americans. So yes, we would have dominated the world with software exports, just like China dominated the world with manufactured exports.

Education still has problems, as in the rest of the world. Annual Status of Education Reports (ASER) over the last two decades have contributed an enormous amount to our understanding of the problem – Sita goes to school, but Sita cannot read (at age-appropriate levels). This is near identical to the phenomenon in the US in the mid-1970s – Johnny goes to school, but Johnny cannot read.

True. A recent World Bank report on Learning Poverty breaks up this important aspect of poverty according to two dimensions: schooling deprivation (what per cent of children are going to school) and learning deprivation (what per cent of those in school are not at the age-appropriate levels of learning). A combination of these two indices yields an index (in percentages) of learning poverty. And learning poverty differences across countries makes for informed learning.

What does this comparative analysis show (Table 10.2)? That learning poverty in India is 54.8%, with schooling deprivation now down to just 2.3% – i.e. everybody is going to school. Learning deprivation is for more than half the population, but this too seems to be a problem across many countries. Indonesia has 34%, Brazil has 47% and even a well-educated advanced developing country like Chile has 30%. Vietnam is one of the few countries in the world with a low learning poverty of 1.1%, lower than both the UK and the US.

Table 10.2: Learning Poverty Levels – Selected Countries (%)

Country	Schooling Deprivation	Learning Deprivation	Learning Poverty
Argentina	0.6	53.6	53.9
Bangladesh	4.9	55.0	57.2
Brazil	2.7	46.9	48.4
Chile	9.3	30.3	36.8
China	0.0	18.2	18.2
India	2.3	53.7	54.8
Indonesia	2.4	33.8	35.4
Mexico	1.2	42.5	43.2
Pakistan	27.3	65.0	74.5
South Africa	8.4	77.9	79.8
Sri Lanka	0.9	14.0	14.8
Thailand	2.0	21.9	23.5
UK	0.2	3.2	3.4
Uruguay	0.5	41.4	41.7
US	4.1	3.9	7.9
Vietnam	0.6	1.1	1.7

Source: Joao Pedro Azevedo, *Learning Poverty: Measures and Simulations*, https://doi.org/10.1596/1813-9450-9446, 2020

The comparative picture is illustrative. The bad news is that we have a problem we have known about for a long time, thanks to ASER. The not-so-bad news is that we have company – lots of it.

11

Redistribution with Growth

In the early 1970s, President McNamara of the World Bank initiated a study to guide the bank on its policies towards economic development. Outside of the Western economies and Japan, the whole world was poor, dirt poor. The 'policy' book was called *Redistribution with Growth*, authored by India's own Montek S. Ahluwalia along with Nick Carter and Hollis Chenery. Since then, economists and policymakers around the world (and economists at the World Bank!) have been chasing the ephemeral dream of Redistribution with Growth.

There have been several growth successes – China, Vietnam, Korea, Indonesia to name a few. But 'Redistribution with Growth' requires both growth and at the least a stable level of inequality or, better still, a decline in inequality.

In the previous chapters we have seen how employment has advanced and poverty has declined; at record levels for India, and where poverty decline is concerned, it is close to the fastest rates in the world and more than comparable to the best in the world such as Vietnam. A recent IMF staff paper, Elif Arbatli-Saxegaard et al. (2023)[1] concur with the thrust of our findings, and document how both poverty and inequality in India have declined since 2015.

How was this equity achieved? Through a combination of growth and taxation. As shown in Bhalla (2022), *total* government tax revenue (centre, state and local) amounting to around 17% of GDP, as computed by the IMF, was higher than the average for most emerging markets. These data are somewhat dated (only until 2019).

The tax–GDP ratio for India for 2022–23 is close to 19%, if not higher. A summary of individual-level tax data (see Ghosh 2023 and our own preliminary analysis) shows that the individual income tax base (those who file returns) has also expanded enormously. Between 2011 and 2020, the number of those who *filed returns* increased from 46 million to 87 million; the number of those who *paid taxes* (i.e. declared incomes greater than ₹2.5 lakh per annum) more than quadrupled from 14 million in 2011–12 period to 57 million in the 2020–21 period.

No matter the prism used to dissect the numbers, the tax and redistribution record in India is impressive, and it has vastly improved over the last decade. But did this redistribution happen *with growth*? Here it is tragically amusing for scholars (and their narratives) to point to the second term of Modi as a 'failure'.

Let the record state that, between 2019 and 2023, India grew at a lower-than-expected 4.1% per annum. In the first

Modi term 2014–18, GDP growth topped 7.1%. The second Modi term was also witness to the greatest worldwide shock since World War II – Covid-19. Most scholars (and policymakers) would chalk up the Covid shock as an extreme outlier and move on. Which is what India has done very successfully. Ignoring this one-off 'manna from hell', India grew at 6.6% per annum, and in the last few years, it has been a G20 economy with the fastest growth and possibly the fastest major economy in the world. And the IMF World Economic Outlook (WEO) expects this resurgent trend to continue for at least the next five years.

However, it is not the growth that has been so remarkable under circumstances of adversity (Covid and slower worldwide growth) but the redistribution that has accompanied it. The redistribution is not the fictional one invented by the 2017–18 CES, but a genuine and successful attempt to improve the lives of the bottom half of the population. India used to spend 4–5% of GDP on leaky subsidies, and most of these were of the non-merit kind. Now, DBT-targeted subsidies and an efficiently run public distribution system (PDS) mean that 3% of GDP is being well targeted at those who need them.

Indeed, if a reform is needed, it is in breaking up the official alliance between the minimum support price (MSP) of foodgrains and the PDS. Surely a better system exists? Use technology to give cash transfers to both consumers and producers, and let the farmer produce and sell what she wants to, and let the consumer buy lentils or fruits or vegetables (or even a soda) from the money she saves by not being 'forced' to eat 10 kg of grains per month. Stop looking for inefficient markets to offload the surplus grain.

Back to inequality. Surprise, surprise. The government has (again) delayed the release of the consumer expenditure data for 2022–23, so a direct comparison with the 2011–12 data is not possible. The release of the CES 2022–23 data will inform us both about what has happened in the preceding 11 years, and whether the quality of data is back to the normality that existed before the 2017–18 Titanic disaster. As we go to print release of the CES 2022–23 survey, results confirm that quality of data is back to 2011–12 levels! Maybe we will also have an official commentary and analysis by the government's expert group on what really happened in 2017–18. One can only hope for this.

But we cannot wait for Godot before reaching some broad conclusions about growth and equity since 2004–05. The first four decades after Independence our economy was weak, and per capita growth was low or non-existent. Today, and for the last 30 years, the economy has grown in a robust manner. The selection debate today is not around Left versus Right or socialism versus capitalism. It is which ten-year regime – UPA 2004 to 2013 or BJP-led NDA 2014 to 2023 – has delivered greater welfare improvement and higher, more sustainable growth. What distinguishes one regime from another? We will provide data and attempt an answer.

In Table 8.1 it was shown that employment growth between 2004–05 and 2017–18 was the slowest ever in Indian history (data available since 1983). Only about 1.3 million jobs per year were created over 13 years (10 years of which were in the UPA period). Since 2017–18, over the last five years, an average of 13.6 million jobs per year have been created, out of which 8 million per year were paid jobs.

But what happened to real wages?

Table 11.1: Real Wage Levels and Growth in India – 1999/2000–2022/23

	Rural India		All India		
	Crops only	All Agriculture	Casual	Salaried	Self-employed
Per Worker Per Day Wages – 2011/12 prices					
1999	71.6	71.8	84.4	309.2	
2004	77.8	78.5	92.8	301.7	
2011	120.1	121.7	142.2	394.1	
2017	144.8	147.7	177.8	357.4	258.0
2018	151.6	154.9	188.0	349.3	263.2
2019	147.0	148.6	182.7	345.8	249.1
2020	150.7	153.9	189.6	343.5	242.4
2021	171.5	176.3	214.9	348.5	260.3
2022	170.0	172.9	218.2	341.1	275.9
CAG Growth – % Per Annum					
2004–11	6.2	6.3	6.1	3.8	
2017–22	3.2	3.2	4.1	-0.9	1.3

Sources: 1999–2011 NSSO, 2017–22 PLFS; CPIAL and CPIIW data on consumer prices
Note: Real wages derived by deflating nominal wages by CPIAL (rural areas) and urban wages by CPIIW.

175

Here there is an interesting equity story. Table 11.1 shows what has happened to real wages in agriculture, and all of India. Despite the narrative that real agricultural wages have declined, rural distress, the K-shaped recovery and all that jazz, NSSO/PLFS data suggest that wages in agriculture are growing at a robust pace (upwards of 3% per annum). However, this pace has declined from about 6% per annum earlier.

Table 11.1 also shows that casual worker wages are expanding at a rapid pace of 4.1% per annum. Casual (and agricultural) workers have the lowest wage among the three categories of workers for whom wage data are gathered by PLFS. The survey asks detailed questions for casual work and wages but only one question of salaried workers: How much did you make last month? Since 2017–18 it also asks that one question of self-employed workers. Prior to 2017–18, salaried workers also were asked several questions about their jobs.

Notwithstanding questions about data quality, the data suggests that the real wages of salaried workers have been stagnant since 2017 (marginal decline of 1% a year), while for self-employed, real wages have risen at an annual 1.3% pace. There's been a huge expansion in taxpayers and tax payments, and this has occurred at a pace much, much faster than per capita GDP growth. The preliminary estimate of real taxpayer income growth is that their taxable income has grown at a rate of 1.7% per annum. Part of this may be a formalization of earlier work that previously lay outside the tax net. Nevertheless, with salaried individuals also showing real growth in their incomes, the overall conclusion is that all sectors have shown real growth, and that the poorest set of worker wages have increased at a faster pace. This is equitable growth. Add to it the fact that income taxes are paid by the upper 25% of workers, the reality is that what has been observed in India is Redistribution with growth.

But while it is difficult to glean the 'exact' details about the trends in income distribution in India (work and research on this is well under way!), it is very likely that income inequality has more than moderately declined in the last decade. And, by the way, some knowledge about income distribution is essential if we want to be an upper-income advanced developed nation.

So when will PLFS conduct an income distribution survey? (I had suggested precisely this more than 15 years ago as a member of the first National Statistical Commission.) Without this, we're reduced to guesswork, informed though it may be.

It is true that real wage growth has slowed post 2017, and this has been accompanied by an unprecedented expansion of employment. Quantity meets price, which is classic Economics 101. High employment growth and low real wage growth. The earlier period (2004–11) was an 'elite' period – privileged workers with jobs and a scarcity of employment. Again, Econ 101. Low supply, excess demand, and real wages rising at a faster rate.

If we are concerned with welfare and voting behaviour, surely inclusive growth 2014–24 is better than the exclusive 2004–13 growth we saw earlier?

Aggregate macro growth over the last two decades

In Chapter 2 we tried to connect the dots between electoral triumph and the economy. We noted that there seemed to be a reasonable connection. As India goes to the polls, what the pundits are talking about is relative economic performance. That is a vindication of our long-held view that the economy is a prime determinant of electoral fortune.

This is not a new idea. James Carville popularized it with his quip 'It is the Economy, Stupid', which Bill Clinton adopted in 1992. But it was a young professor at Princeton, Ray Fair, who estimated the first econometric model relating electoral outcomes to incumbency and two economic variables – unemployment and inflation. I was a graduate student at Princeton when Ray Fair developed his model and I learnt from him!

The learning continues to this day, and I have resisted all diversions from the main focus – it is emphatically not caste, nor is it gender, nor is it ideology. Individuals are rational economic agents and the choice of their leader is a function of how good he or she would be for their economic welfare.

Polemics aside, let us look at the record of economic growth 2004 to 2023

First, as an intelligent voter, some ground rules. The first rule of comparison is what Karan Bhasin and I invoked – no country is an island any more, and hence the comparison must explicitly take into account the external environment. A rising tide lifts all boats and exaggerates all growth rates (what happened in 2004–13). The following is largely based on a Bhalla-Bhasin article 'Whose Economic Performance Was Better, UPA or NDA? Growth Rates Don't Tell the Whole Story'.[2]

Both the periods, 2004–13 and 2014–23, experienced a global recession, the second one more severe than the first. If they were of equal severity, then there would be no reason to drop either year from the analysis. However, the 2020–21 pandemic had a much greater intensity of shock relative to the global financial crisis. (Parenthetically, India and China were not that much affected by the first shock.) Indeed, the pandemic was the greatest global shock since World War II. As the least bad comparison, we decided to omit the two outlier growth years, 2008–09 and 2020–21, from our analysis.

What do the results show? But looks can be deceptive.

India's GDP growth was 7.8% per annum between 2004 and 2013 and a lower 6.9% per annum between 2014 and 2023. Population weighted average global growth (excluding India) was 5.6% per annum 2004–13, the highest ever recorded in post-War world history; a rising tide if ever there was one and a tide that very quickly faded. India's excess growth over global growth during this period was a healthy 2.2% a year. We did well, very well during 2004–13. But India grew even faster, relative to the rest of the world, during 2014–23, when it exceeded global growth by an even healthier 2.9% excess. This is given by India's growth of 6.9% versus world growth of 4%.

Briefly summarizing, wage, income and employment data show the following: Growth has been continuing since 1991 and all governments did well and deserve our gratitude and applause. But even if you like two candidates in an election, you have to make one choice. Both the excess growth and inclusive nature of growth indicate that the odds (or our preference function) are heavily tilted in favour of Modi in Choice 2024.

Modi's forecasts and expectations: US$5 trillion by 2025 and developed economy by 2047

A hallmark of PM Modi is that he is not hesitant to make forecasts on the economy. Earlier we had discussed how the narrative experts had attempted to ridicule Modi for his 'promise' of creating 10 million jobs a year. It turns out he was massively right – more jobs have been created in the last 10 years than ever before, and significantly more than an average of 10 million a year.

In his second term, there are two prominent forecasts/ expectations that Mr Modi has made public. First, India will be a US$5 trillion economy by 2025, and second, we should aim for a developed country status by our Independence centenary year 2047.

In October 2018, a task force set up by the government made the following recommendation: 'The underlying strengths are indicative of the potential of India to achieve a US$5 trillion economy by 2025.' There is a delicious ambiguity in the data – is it December 2025 or the end of fiscal year 2025–26 (India's fiscal year runs from April to March). The latter interpretation gives an extra three months to reach the target. At this point, the distinction is academic; GDP for fiscal year 2023–24 is likely to be close to $3.7 trillion, a good 35% away from its target in 2025–26. Assuming no change in the rupee–dollar exchange rate from its 82.6 average in 2023 and a 10% increase in nominal dollar GDP in each of the next two years, India's dollar GDP would still be around $4.5 trillion in 2025–26 (April 2025 to March 2026). With these assumptions, April–December 2026 is a more likely date for India's tryst with $5 trillion.

How come the Modi administration got the GDP $5

trillion forecast so wrong? Well, they did, but they didn't get it all that wrong. At the time the forecast was made (October 2018), the Indian economy was coasting at around $2.7 trillion. Demonetization had come and gone, and in 2017–18, dollar GDP expanded at a 15.5% rate. And then came Covid, a worldwide shock. Given that there was a Covid shock and extra currency depreciation, to reach the target one year later is impressive in terms of the original forecast.

India and China – twins with paths converging – both to be advanced economies by 2047 (and India more so because of socio-democratic variables)

To paraphrase Jane Austen, it is now a truth universally acknowledged that Indian GDP growth is the fastest among the G20 economies and is expected to be so over the course of this decade. Geopolitics has turned attention away from China – and towards India.

Economics is responsible for this change, not geopolitics. In 2019, Indian PPP per capita incomes were 47.5% of China's. We estimate that convergence in per capita income *levels* for India and China is very possible (and latest) by 2044 (see Bhalla-Bhasin 2023).[3]

This means that per capita *growth* rates in India should be higher than China on a sustained basis. A little-known fact is that this had already started to happen in the previous decade. Between 2010 and 2019, per capita GDP growth in India was *higher* than in China: 5.2% vs 4.5%. *This marked the first decade after the 1960s when India grew faster than China.*

Convergence means the two incomes should be equal. What will make the long road from 47.5% to 100% possible? Each determinant of growth (labour, capital, human capital and total factor productivity or TFP) will likely play a part.

A conservative conclusion – India will grow at an average 3.5% faster rate than China in the 2020–45 interval. If it does, India will be a developed country in 2047, as will China

The long history of convergence favours India. For approximately 480 years (between 1500 and 1980) China and India had the same per capita income (constant PPP $). Then came the big divergence for 44 years; at its peak, in 2014, China's per capita income was 2.34 times that of India. History does repeat itself, sometimes in a V-shaped pattern. The path to reconvergence is likely to take less than 30 years.

The critics have entered into various debates as to the definition of developed economy, etc., and have complicated the calculations. There is a simple Occam's Razor estimate. Today, circa 2024, GDP per capita in US dollar terms is close to US $2850 per capita. Assume *nominal* GDP grows at a conservative rate of only 9.5% per annum, per capita GDP growth would then be 8.5% per annum. Assume further, again very conservative, a depreciation of the rupee at 0.5% per annum. (Very likely, the rupee will appreciate, not depreciate, over the next two decades.) The ultra-conservative assumption of an average depreciation of 0.5% per-year yields 8% per capita dollar GDP growth or a level of US$16,730 in 2047. The entry-level for developed country status today (World Bank high income) is US$13205.

But a developed country is about more than income. Yes. It means medical advancement, education advancement, female pilots, a high ratio of women researchers in STEM, etc. For most countries (except oil-rich economies) dollar income advancement lags behind social indicator development. Finally, India has been a successful democracy for the last 75 years. India achieving developed country status by 2047 is one of the safest bets on board.

12

Not Forecast 2024, But . . .[1]

Only fools and psephologists make forecasts, and while we claim to be neither, we can't resist the temptation to stick our necks out. Given the amount of betting that takes place in cricket (large sums are wagered on outcomes like 'Who will bowl the next over? On which ball will the next boundary come?'), we feel that a tentative forecast is entirely appropriate. The Chinese have an ancient saying 'Crossing the river by feeling the stones' and this forecast is in that spirit of caution – a feeling of the stones.

The dominant story in the 2024 election is whether the BJP, and Prime Minister Modi, will win three elections in a row. For the BJP, it is a remarkable transformation from the 2 seats it won in 1984. It has been an equal but opposite transformation from what happened in 1984. In an unprecedented victory, with near 50% of the votes and 415 seats, the Congress is now fighting to retain the tag of single largest Opposition party, having won just 44 seats in 2014 and 52 seats in 2019.

What is common to both these transformations is the year

1989. It turns out that 1989 was also an important political year for the world. We want to digress a little bit into that space, before getting back to the BJP and the Congress.

The importance of 1989

It was Lenin who said, 'There are decades where nothing happens; and there are weeks where decades happen.' The popular saying 'A week is a long time in politics' does not quite have the appeal of Lenin's pithy description. The year 1989 was one such in terms of the number of global transformative changes that happened – political and technological.

President Ronald Reagan had earlier issued a directive making Global Positioning System (GPS), once it was sufficiently developed, freely available for civilian use as a common 'public' good. On 14 February, the first GPS satellite was launched into orbit. On 13 March, Tim Berners-Lee invented the World Wide Web as a way of sharing information between computers. The first babies born after pre-implantation genetic diagnosis were conceived in late 1989. Genetic modification of adult human beings was tried for the first time, in a gene-tagging trial.

On 15 February, the long-drawn Soviet–Afghan war ended as the last Soviet Union troops left Kabul, ending their decade-old military occupation. In the summer, Mikhail Gorbachev visited China, the first Soviet leader to do so since Nikita Khrushchev in the 1960s, thus 'ending' the Sino-Soviet split. Post Gorbachev's visit, China witnessed the 1989 Tiananmen Square protests in which a 10-metre-high 'Goddess of Democracy' statue was unveiled in Tiananmen Square by student demonstrators. In Iran, the First Supreme Leader Ayatollah Khomeini issued a fatwa against Salman Rushdie for his book *The Satanic Verses* on charges of blasphemy. Khomeini's death in June 1989, at the age of 89, led to eight people being killed and hundreds injured in a human crush during the viewing of his body in Tehran. The year ended with the fall of the Berlin Wall on 9 November and for the first time in decades, East Germany opened checkpoints to allow its citizens to travel freely to West Germany.

Importance of 1989 for India

Meanwhile in India. After winning the largest mandate in Indian elections in 1984, Rajiv Gandhi tumbled to an embarrassing defeat in 1989. Prior to the elections, in the relatively quiet hill station of Palampur in the northern state of Himachal Pradesh, the BJP's national executive passed a resolution to build the Ram Temple at Ayodhya. It was a defining moment as for the first time a major national political party had openly supported this movement.

The Rath Yatra from Somnath to Ayodhya began in September 1990; it was meant to mobilize support for the cause of the Ayodhya temple. L.K. Advani, the BJP leader and initiator of the Rath Yatra, who was recently awarded the Bharat Ratna, clarified the motives and the historical context behind the yatra and wrote the following in a blog post in 2010: 'The Yatra precipitated in the country a debate: *Genuine* Secularism versus *Pseudo* Secularism – a debate that had first come to the fore forty years earlier when Pandit Nehru had reprimanded Dr. Munshi for his activity related to Somnath.'[2] Advani was referring to an incident in which India's first prime minister Jawaharlal Nehru had told off his then cabinet minister Dr Munshi, saying, 'I don't like your trying to restore Somnath. It is Hindu revivalism.' Advani writes how Dr Munshi recalled the first President Dr Rajendra Prasad who took the opposite stance to Nehru's stating that he (Prasad) would come and install the deity whatever the attitude of the prime minister. Prasad further added, 'I would do the same with a mosque or church if I were invited.' Munshi using this example as a crucial dividing line, particularly with the politics of the then ruling class represented by Prime Minister Nehru, declaratively stated '. . . this, he (then President Prasad) held, was the core of Indian secularism. Our State is neither religious nor anti-religious.'[3]

Advani, in the same blog post, traces the roots of the Ayodhya issue to Swami Vivekananda who in his book *The Future of India* wrote, 'Temple after temple was broken down by the foreign conqueror, but no sooner had the wave passed than the spire of the temple rose up again. Some of these old temples of South India, and those like Somnath in Gujarat, will teach you volumes of wisdom, which will give you a keener insight into the history of the race than any amount of books. Mark how these temples bear the marks of a hundred attacks and a hundred regenerations, continually destroyed and continually springing up out of the ruins, rejuvenated and strong as ever! That is the national mind, that is the national life-current. Follow it and it leads to glory.' Following this, Advani says, 'It is therefore only natural that, when India became independent, many Hindus felt that 1947 should signify not only freedom from British rule but also a clean break from those aspects of the pre-British history that were identified with subjugation, assaults on Hindu temples, vandalizing idols and erosion of our noble cultural traditions.'[4]

By explicitly emphasizing the difference between genuine secularism and psuedo secularism, Advani articulated his disapproval of the practice of secularism, not the spirit behind it. No matter to what extent one agrees or disagrees with Advani's version of history and politics, events since 1989 seem to have vindicated most of what he had envisaged paralleling the rise of the BJP as the predominant national uniparty in a new India. We will soon look at the statistical evidence for the same.

The 2004 election and non leap-year parallels with 2024

As a first step in that direction, we want to review what happened in 2004. In that year, India had just started to shine and the BJP was expected to win the election but it lost. The Opposition today is busy reminding all that history will repeat itself. The chances of that happening is what this chapter is all about.

The Congress decline was coincident with the emergence of strong regional parties in the national arena, which eventually led to the formation of the United Progressive Alliance or UPA-I. The formation of the I.N.D.I.A. block in the forthcoming election with Congress as its figurehead and a potpourri of regional parties therefore logically leads to the following question – can 2024 be a repeat of 2004, as both are leap years?!

Ahead of the 2004 elections, there was a notable effort to form a Congress-led national-level joint Opposition front. However, despite these attempts, a comprehensive agreement could not be reached. Instead of a pan-India alliance, the Congress forged regional alliances with various parties in different states. In Uttar Pradesh, the largest state in India by population, both the Bahujan Samajwadi Party and the Samajwadi Party, two influential and then ascending political entities, chose not to align with the

Congress. The left parties, particularly the CPM and the Communist Party of India (CPI), contested independently in their strongholds such as West Bengal, Tripura and Kerala, where they confronted both Congress and NDA forces. In states like Punjab and Andhra Pradesh, they engaged in seat-sharing arrangements with the Congress.

Several hypotheses have been put forward to explain the BJP-led NDA's loss in the 2004 elections. Factors such as the electorate's rejection of the BJP's 'India Shining' campaign and the RSS's perceived lack of enthusiasm in supporting the BJP, among others, have been suggested. It is difficult to conclusively identify the cause of the BJP's 2004 loss, except to note the following three facts. First, contrary to the overall decline in the seat count, the BJP actually *gained* 11 seats in the southern state of Karnataka. Moreover, the party performed comparatively well in Odisha, Maharashtra, Madhya Pradesh, the newly created Chhattisgarh, and the western states of Punjab and Rajasthan.

Second, and more importantly, in the crucial battleground states of Uttar Pradesh and Bihar, the BJP significantly underperformed relative to the 1999 election. Thirty-seven seats were lost in just these two states. Third, in three northern states (Delhi, Gujarat and Haryana) the BJP lost 16 seats relative to 1999. Table 12.1 contains the results.

Table 12.1: BJP's Performance in 1999 and 2004 Lok Sabha Elections

State	1999 Contested	Won	2004 Contested	Won	Seats Loss/ Gain
Uttar Pradesh	77	29	77	10	-19
Bihar	29	23	16	5	-18
Jharkhand			14	1	1
Delhi	7	7	7	1	-6
Gujarat	26	20	26	14	-6
Haryana	5	5	10	1	-4
Andhra Pradesh	8	7	9	0	-7
Tamil Nadu	6	4	6	0	-4
Madhya Pradesh	40	29	29	25	-4
Chhattisgarh			11	10	10
Punjab	3	1	3	3	2
Rajasthan	24	16	25	21	5
Maharashtra	26	13	26	13	0
Odisha	9	9	9	7	-2
Karnataka	19	7	24	18	11
Total	339	182	364	138	-44

Source: Election Commission of India

Note: Jharkhand and Chhattisgarh were newly created in 2000 majorly from Bihar and Madhya Pradesh and therefore have to be analysed together.

Comparing BJP's winning margins in 2019 and 2004

Some clues as to whether 2024 will be a repeat of 2004 (for the anti-BJP alliance) can be obtained from the distribution of the winning margins in Bihar and UP in the 2004 and

2019 election. There is an important difference – in 2019, the BJP had significantly strengthened its position in the northern heartland states compared to its margins in the 1999 election. To highlight this contrast, we present the distribution of the BJP's winning margins in UP and Bihar in Figure 12.1. The horizontal axis represents the winning margin (presented in buckets of 5% such as 0 to 5%, 5+ to 10%, etc.) while the vertical axis represents the percentage of seats won within the margin of a given bucket.

In 2004, the BJP was in a more precarious situation, with winning margins of 5% or below in 24 out of the 52 seats in the Hindi heartland, indicating a relatively high share of vulnerable seats. However, by 2019, the political landscape had evolved, and the BJP enjoyed robust margins across the majority of seats, making a substantial swing against the party in these states an improbable scenario in the 2024 general election.

The stark contrast in the winning margins between 1999 and 2019 exemplifies the party's enhanced electoral performance in 2019. As a result, the BJP's current standing in these heartland states presents a formidable electoral advantage, signalling a significant departure from the vulnerabilities it faced in 2004.

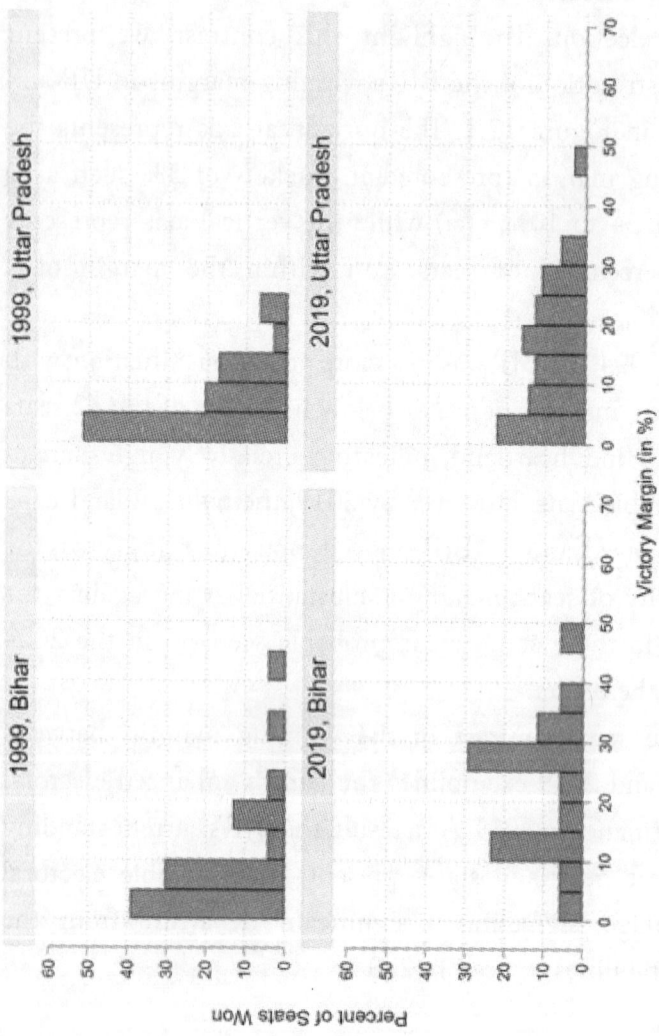

Figure 12.1: Distribution of BJP's Margin of Victory for the Winning Seats in Uttar Pradesh and Bihar in 1999 and 2019

The decline and decline of the Congress

It seems that India has always had a one and a half national party system – one dominant national party, with a host of regional parties providing alliances and the checks and balances. Even during the dominant early years of Nehru, the Congress party could only muster a peak 47.8% vote share in the Lok Sabha elections in 1957. In 1984, the BJP won just 2 seats. In the 1989 election, it won 86. In 2019, the BJP won 303 seats, and the Congress won 54. Can one connect the dots in the swings? We can as we will now demonstrate.

But first the 'electoral' picture of the two national parties, the Congress and the BJP, from 1952 to the present (Tables 12.2a and 12.2b). Pay particular attention to the national vote shares and their trend. First the Congress, which split in 1967 and was reinvented as the Indian National Congress (Indira Gandhi), INC. From a peak vote share in 1957 of 47.8% (ignoring the outlier election of 1984) the Congress vote share declined to only 19.3% in 2014, and 19.5% in 2019.

Table 12.2a: Performance in Lok Sabha Elections – INC

| Year | Seats | | National Vote Share (%) |
	Contested	Won	
1952	479	364	45.0
1957	490	371	47.8
1962	488	361	44.7

Year	Seats		National Vote Share (%)
	Contested	Won	
1967	516	283	40.8
1971	441	352	43.7
1977	492	154	34.5
1980	492	353	42.7
1984	491	414	49.1
1989	510	197	39.5
1991	487	232	36.3
1996	529	140	28.8
1998	477	141	25.8
1999	453	114	28.3
2004	417	145	26.5
2009	440	206	28.6
2014	464	44	19.3
2019	421	52	19.5

Source: Election Commission of India

Note: Indira Gandhi breakaway Congress INC(I) which contested in the 1980 election is recoded as INC.

Figure 12.1(a) plots the trend of the Congress vote share over the last 70 years. This is a strong trend of -0.42% per annum (omitting the 1984 outlier year) revealing a decline in the Congress vote share of just above 2 percentage points every five years. This is revealed by the trend coefficient of 0.42; the explanatory power of the model is very high at 0.88 (Table 12.3).

India has changed enormously over the last 70 years – in politics and economics. Coalitions have come and gone – and since 1991 economic reforms have been dominant, except for reform-slumber between 2004 and 2013. But

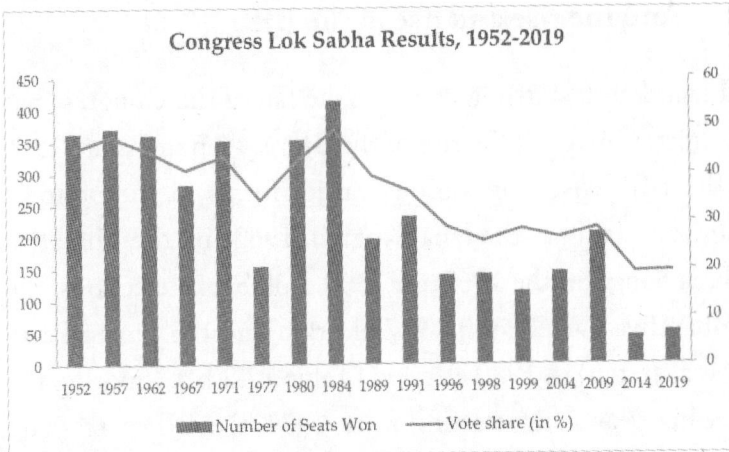

Figure 12.1(a): Congress Party Lok Sabha Results

what Figure 12.1 shows is that the Congress decline is 'constant like the Northern star, of whose true fixed and resting quality there is no fellow in the firmament'.

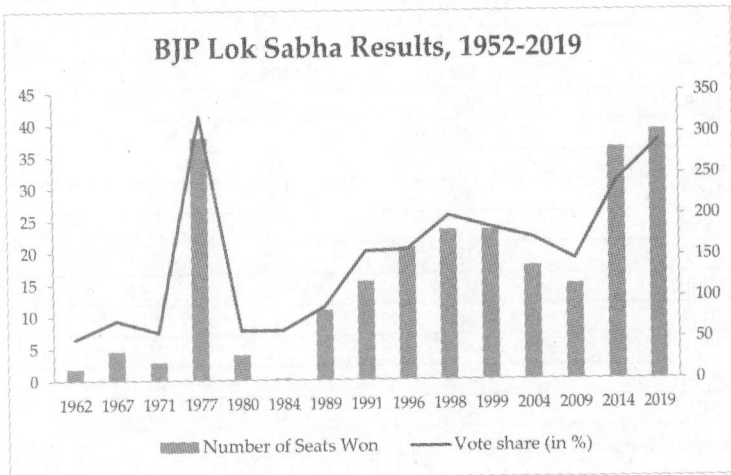

Figure 12.2: BJP Lok Sabha Results

... And the rise and rise of the BJP

In stark and startling contrast, the fall of the Congress has a mirror image of the rise of the BJP as seen in Figure 12.2. The BJP existed in various earlier forms in the political arena starting as the Jana Sangh in 1962 and the Bharatiya Jana Sangh in the 1967 and 1971 Lok Sabha elections; the Bharatiya Lok Dal in 1977 election and the Janata Party (at a stretch) in 1980 election (Table 12.2(b)). Ignoring the earlier years, and starting from 1984, the BJP vote share shows a strong trend increase, even stronger than the trend decline of the Congress.

Table 12.2b: Performance in Lok Sabha Elections – BJP

Year	Seats		National Vote Share (%)
	Contested	Won	
1962	196	14	6.4
1967	249	35	9.3
1971	157	22	7.4
1977	405	295	41.3*
1980	433	31	7.7
1984	224	2	7.7
1989	225	85	11.4
1991	468	120	20.1
1996	471	161	20.3
1998	388	182	25.6
1999	339	182	23.8
2004	364	138	22.2
2009	433	116	18.8
2014	428	282	31.0
2019	436	303	37.3

Source: Election Commission of India; author's calculations.
Note: *Jana Sangh in 1962, Bharatiya Jana Sangh in 1967 and 1971, Bharatiya Lok Dal in 1977 and Janata Party in 1980 are recoded as the BJP.

Outlier election years: If we plot vote shares over time, we find that there is a clear trend where the Congress vote share declines (with that one huge spike in 1984 being the exception). Conversely, we find that the BJP's vote share rises over time (with the post-Emergency 1977 elections when the ancestor of the BJP was in an alliance with several other parties being an exception). Both the decline (INC) and the rise (BJP) are predictable using a simple statistical technique called regression analysis. In the BJP's case, one needs a dummy variable to account for the multi-party alliance against the Congress in 1977. In the case of the INC, the assassination-induced outlandish victory in 1984 is a very eligible dummy. Dummy variables factor out exceptional data that distorts the usual relationship and help us estimate the normal time trend while accounting for the outlier values.

In Table 12.3, we present results from three regressions that are henceforth referred to as 'time trend' models. In order to predict the national vote shares of the INC and the BJP, we use the vote share in the election year as a dependent variable, time (and outlier dummies) as independent variables.

Figures 12.3(a), 12.3(b) and 12.3(c) present the 'added variable plots' from the three regressions reported in Table 12.3. (An added variable plot is a graph of the vote share with time after netting out the influence of the time dummy variables.) The figures show the long-run time trends in the

Table 12.3: Results from Time Trend Models for INC and BJP

| | National Vote Share | | |
	INC	BJP	BJP LR1
Year	-0.42***	0.74***	0.46***
d1984	13.54**		
d2009		-10.52*	
d1977			29.61***
# Observations	17	10	15
R2 Adj.	0.87	0.85	0.81

Sources: Election Commission of India; author's calculations.

Notes:

1) BJP Long run (LR) refers to the time trend model for the BJP starting 1962.
2) Reported coefficients are significant at + p < 0.1, * p < 0.05, ** p < 0.01, *** p < 0.001

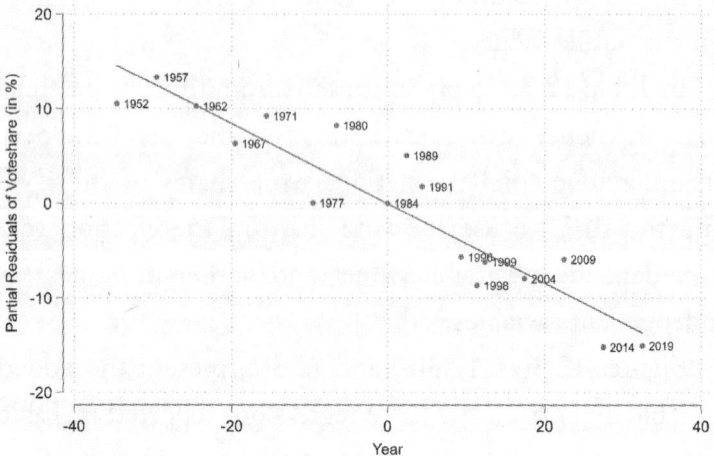

coef = -.42105256, se = .04340414, t = -9.7
Note: *The X-axis represents year controlled for the 1984 outlier election year as a dummy variable.*

Figure 12.3(a) – AVPlot from Time Trend model for INC

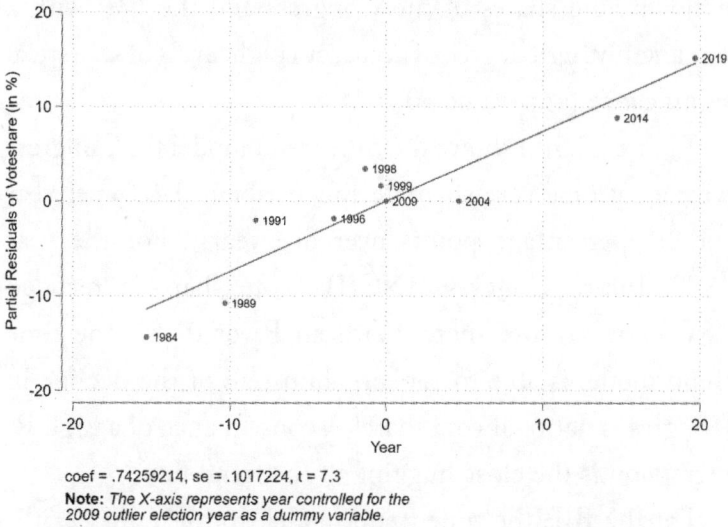

coef = .74259214, se = .1017224, t = 7.3
Note: *The X-axis represents year controlled for the 2009 outlier election year as a dummy variable.*

Figure 12.3(b) – AVPlot from Time Trend model for BJP

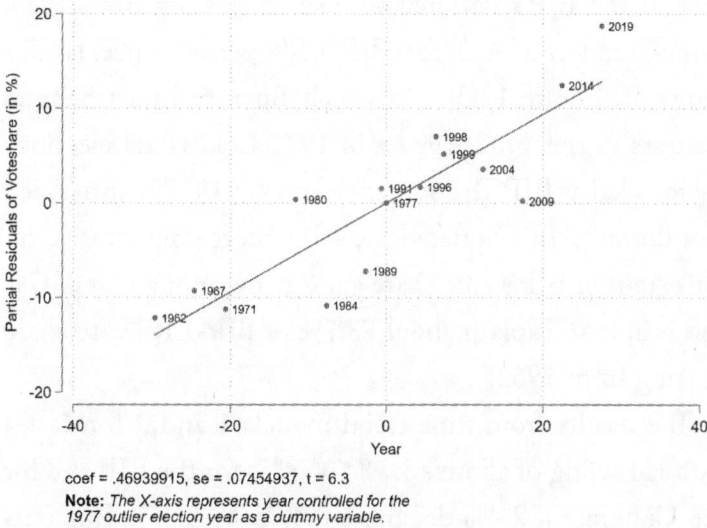

coef = .46939915, se = .07454937, t = 6.3
Note: *The X-axis represents year controlled for the 1977 outlier election year as a dummy variable.*

Figure 12.3(c) – AVPlot from Time Trend model for BJP-LR

national vote shares of the Congress and the BJP with a remarkably high degree of accuracy (high levels of statistical significance (at p-value <0.001).

Figure 12.3(a) shows the time trend model for Congress with a national vote share decline of about 0.42% per year (or 2.1 percentage points over five years). For the year 1980, Indira Congress INC(I)'s vote share is recoded as Congress's vote share. With an R^2 of 0.887, the time trend model is able to explain almost all of the decline in Congress's national vote share! A consequence of a high R^2 regression is the close hugging of the trend line.

For the BJP, the time trend model from Figure 12.3(b) suggests an annual vote share increase of about 0.74%. The time trend model for the BJP is also able to explain about 88% of the BJP's national vote share starting from 1989. Time trend model 3 for BJP-LR's performance is also shown in Figure 12.3(c) in which Bharatiya Jana Sangh's contests in the 1962, 1967 and 1971 Lok Sabha elections are recoded as BJP. The outlier election of 1977 is also coded as a dummy. This updated model is more conservative on the extent of BJP's vote share gains per year of about 0.47% and is able to explain about 83.7% of BJP-LR's vote share starting from 1962.

The results from time trend models 1 and 2 forecast a national swing of about +3.7% (0.74*5) for the BJP and for the Congress a 2.4% decline (-0.47*5 = -2.35). This puts the BJP at 41% and the Congress at about 17% in the 2024 election. This is our first clue towards interpreting and/or forecasting the election.

Note that this mathematical calculation tells us nothing about *why* these two trends have occurred. All we can say is that these patterns have been sustained over a very long period of time – and they seem to have a high degree of predictability.

Could this pattern break? Of course. But the only years in which it has broken – in 1977 and 1984 – have involved extraordinary circumstances. In the absence of such extraordinary circumstances, it is reasonable to assume these trends will continue.

Back to the future – the I.N.D.I.A. partnership-in-waiting

At the time we are writing this, the Indian National Developmental Inclusive Alliance (I.N.D.I.A.) comprises 20 major parties, collectively commanding a strength of 137 seats in the current Lok Sabha. In Bihar, JD(U) supremo Nitish Kumar dumped the alliance for the NDA in 2024 and, in the process, resigned and was reappointed as the chief minister of the state for the ninth time – all in just three days. This one move ahead of the all-important Lok Sabha elections has earned Nitish the moniker *Palturam* (chameleon) among Indian politicians. But why would the usually politically savvy Nitish knowingly risk such a move back to the NDA, potentially jeopardizing his fate

not just in the national election but also in the 2025 Bihar
assembly elections?

**Table 12.4: I.N.D.I.A. Block – 2024 Parties' Performance
in 2019**

Party	National Vote Share (%)	Contested	2019 Won[1]	2024 Alliance[2]
Congress	19.7	402	52	61
All India Trinamool Congress	4.1	47	22	18
Samajwadi Party (SP)	2.6	39	5	3
Dravida Munnetra Kazhagam (DMK)	2.3	24	24	24
National Congress Party (NCP)	1.4	23	5	5
Rashtriya Janata Dal	1.1	21	0	6
Janata Dal (United)	1.5	18	16	7
Communist Party of India (CPI)	0.6	35	2	8
Aam Aadmi Party (AAP)	0.4	25	1	6
All Others	1.4	29	10	11
I.N.D.I.A - Total	35.0	663	137	149

Sources: Election Commission of India, news reports; author's calculations.
Notes:
1) 2019 'Won' column refers to the number of seats in the 2019–24 Lok Sabha.
2) The 2024 'Alliance' column refers to the seats each party would have got if they had fought together in 2024 without any other changes to the 2019 Lok Sabha election vote share distribution.
3) Seats are allocated to the alliance partners using the highest vote share formula, i.e. in case of more than one alliance partner contesting in a constituency, the seat is allocated to whichever party has received the highest vote share in 2019.

The numbers presented in Table 12.4 suggest that the alliance was doomed from the start. To gauge the potential impact of I.N.D.I.A. as originally envisaged, we conduct a hypothetical exercise by estimating the seats based on the distribution of votes in the 2019 Lok Sabha election.

We then allocate the seats in 2019 based on a ranking of I.N.D.I.A. members' votes. That is, if there was more than one party in any constituency from I.N.D.I.A., the seat would be allocated to the party that obtained the highest vote share in 2019. This is a reasonable assumption and a similar formula was suggested by the regional alliance partners like West Bengal's CM Mamata Banerjee.

The simulation suggests that I.N.D.I.A. would have secured 149 seats – a marginal increase of only 12 seats compared to their 137-seat tally in 2019. This synthetic estimate of 149 seats is likely to be an upper bound as the sum of individual party strengths (sum of the parts) is unlikely to exceed the whole. The change in seats sheds light on the motivations of the alliance partners – the Congress gains 9 seats, and AAP gains 6 seats. The two big losers in the alliance? Janata Dal United (JDU) loses 9 seats and the All India Trinamool Congress (AITC) [Mamata] 4. Is it a real surprise that the two potential losers have bolted?

The modest gain of 12 seats in the hypothetical scenario highlights that while unity can be a strategic advantage, it never guaranteed a significant shift in electoral outcomes unless the Congress improved its head-to-head performance against the BJP, particularly in the Hindi heartland states.

Even prior to Nitish Kumar's *ghar wapsi* (returning home) to the NDA, the electoral landscape in Bihar had undergone significant shifts adding layers of complexity to the political dynamics of the region. Notably, Bihar is the only heartland state to not have had a BJP chief minister so far. The intricate political landscape in Bihar makes electoral predictions a challenging and intriguing task. The state is likely a bellwether, reflecting the intricate dance of alliances and the potential impact of internal party dynamics.

Happenings in 2024 – do assembly results foretell Lok Sabha?

Noted and expert journalist (and part-time psephologist like some of us) Shekhar Gupta in an article in the Print makes a valid point about an emerging narrative on BJP's northern dominance and the painting of a picture of the Indian electorate split into two halves (Gupta, December 2023).

As per Gupta, the theory goes something like this – 'BJP rules the north and the south continues to reject it, and so there exists a horizontal divide in the Indian polity marked by the Vindhyas.'[5] He also goes on to suggest that the 2024 election is not quite a north vs south contest as much as it is about 'the BJP's great limitation in reaching out to the peripheries and coastal states, while it is able to win enough Lok Sabha seats in its own political heartland'. This vulnerability, Gupta says, means that 'the BJP, powerful and all-conquering though it looks, still does not reach anywhere near the pan-Indian pre-eminence the Congress had during the Indira Gandhi era.

As shown in Table 12.4, until the 1984 election, the Congress got seats from across the country and generally remained in the 350-seat ballpark except for the two elections of 1967 and 1977. The Congress also had impressive win rates of above 75% in that era. A closer look at Table 12.4 suggests the BJP has been steadily increasing its win rate over the years. In 2019, the Modi–Shah BJP demolished all opposition in the Hindi states, besides Maharashtra, Gujarat and Karnataka, to reach its highest-ever tally of 303 and a win rate of 72%. The average Congress win rate between 1952 and 1980 (excluding 1967 when the Congress was internally split) was 75%. The BJP came perilously close to this average in 2019. It won 72% of seats contested. Not that unusual if you consider that Congress exceeded or matched that figure in every election between 1952 and 1984 barring the Emergency 1977 election.

Will the BJP exceed the 2019 win rate in 2024? We discuss the maths for 2024 next.

Table 12.5: Winning Parties in Lok Sabha General Elections, 1952–2019

Year	Winning Party	Vote Share (%)	Total	Contested	Won	Win Rate (%)
1952	INC	45.0	489	479	364	76.0
1957	INC	47.8	494	490	371	75.7
1962	INC	44.7	494	488	361	74
1967	INC	40.8	520	516	283	54.8
1971	INC	43.7	518	441	352	79.8
1977	BLD	41.3	542	405	295	72.8
1980	INC	42.7	542	492	353	71.7
1984	INC	49.1	542	491	404	82.3
1989	JD	17.8	543	244	143	58.6
1991	INC	36.3	543	500	232	46.4
1996	BJP	20.3	543	471	161	34.2
1998	INC	25.8	543	477	141	29.6
1999	BJP	23.8	543	339	182	53.7
2004	INC	26.5	543	417	145	34.8
2009	INC	28.6	543	440	206	46.8
2014	BJP	31.0	543	464	282	60.8
2019	BJP	37.3	543	421	303	72.0

Sources: Election Commission of India; author's calculations
Note: Win Rate is calculated as a percentage of seats won to seats contested.

In Table 12.5, we present how the vote shares for the BJP have changed from each assembly election to the next national election. Between 1991 and before the 1996 election, a weighted average of assembly votes for the BJP registered 19.4%. Between 2014 and 2019, the assembly-based *increase* in the vote share for the BJP was 8.8% (from 17.7% in 2009–14 to 26.5% in 2014–19).

Table 12.6: Performance in Lok Sabha Elections Following Assembly Elections, 1991–2024

Time Period		BJP Vote Share (%)		
Assembly	Lok Sabha	Assembly[1]	Lok Sabha	Performance[2]
1991-96	1996	19.4	20.3	0.9
1996-99	1999	30.0	23.8	-6.3
1999-04	2004	18.3	22.2	3.9
2004-09	2009	17.8	18.8	1.0
2009-14	2014	17.7	31.3	13.6
2014-19	2019	26.5	37.5	11.0
2019-24	2024	**31.3**		

Sources: Election Commission of India; author's calculations.
Notes:
1) For assembly elections, the number reported is the weighted average vote shares for the BJP and INC in the assembly elections post the Lok Sabha election. The weights used are the number of Lok Sabha seats in the state.
2) Performance is the change in votes share from Lok Sabha to the assembly elections.

Note also the evolution of the 'Performance' index for the BJP. It is the change in Lok Sabha votes from the preceding assembly elections. For example, between 2014 and 2019 (after Lok Sabha 2014 and *before* Lok Sabha 2019), the BJP assembly vote share (weighted by the share of the state in Lok Sabha seats) was 26.5%. In Lok Sabha 2019, the BJP vote share was 37.5%. The difference between the two

(11 percentage points) is the performance index. It is the evolution of this index that augurs well for the BJP in 2024.

Since 1991, the performance index has averaged 4%, i.e. the average gain in votes from assembly to Lok Sabha has been 4%. Since 1999, the average gain has been a hefty 7.4% (the average of 3.9%, 1%, 13.6% and 11%).

So what does happen in 2024?

Taking our cue from these swing estimates, Table 12.7 attempts to foretell the future. We present simulations, calibrated with swings of 3%, 5% and +7%, both in favour and against each alliance and BJP. It is important to underscore that the swing in favour of either NDA or I.N.D.I.A. does *not* automatically mean a swing against the other (the actual swing is dependent on the distribution of votes in the 2019 election in each Lok Sabha constituency).

Table 12.7: General Elections 2024 Simulations

	LS Current Strength	Swing		
		3	5	7
BJP Only				
Pro Sentiment	303	321	334	347
Anti Sentiment	303	262	234	213
NDA-3				
Pro Sentiment	334	358	370	382
Anti Sentiment	334	291	266	240

	LS Current Strength	Swing		
		3	5	7
I.N.D.I.A.				
Pro Sentiment	133	165	182	207
Anti Sentiment	133	105	97	84

Sources: Election Commission of India; author's calculations.
Notes:
1) Results are reported at the time of JD(U)'s return to the NDA from the I.N.D.I.A. alliance.
2) LS Current Strength is the number of seats in the current (2019–24) Lok Sabha. For the alliances, current strength is the number of the seats each party would have got if they had fought together in 2024 without any other changes to the 2019 Lok Sabha election vote share distribution.
3) Seats are allocated to the I.N.D.I.A. alliance partners using highest vote share formula, i.e. in case of more than one alliance partner contesting in a constituency, the seat is allocated to whichever party has received the highest vote share in 2019.
4) Number of seats for swings is obtained with swings of +-3, 5 and 7 using the 'synthetic' alliances vote share distribution.

The results (with Nitish Kumar back in the NDA): If the BJP vote share increases by 5%, it would likely win 334 seats; with a 7% increase, 347 seats. A 3% increase for I.N.D.I.A. will get it to 165 seats; a 3% decline in its vote share will mean a loss of 28 seats (total equal to only 105). Even a 7% increase in I.N.D.I.A. vote share gets it to only 207 seats – some 65 seats short of a majority and even 2 less than what Manmohan Singh won for the Congress in 2009 alone.

The votes-to-seats maths also makes a major difference in the final outcomes. For instance, in the event of a large anti-incumbency wave in 2024, however unlikely that may seem, the distribution of how the vote is split against the BJP is also important. On the other hand, the BJP is more likely to make major gains if it procures votes from its direct competitors in the respective constituencies. The simulations shown in Table 12.6 from the swing model project a median scenario of BJP gaining equally from the other two candidates who finished in the top three positions in 2019.

As of today, it is unclear as to who remains in the I.N.D.I.A. coalition, how the seats will be shared between parties or if the alliance will collapse entirely. Our analysis gives us a base case scenario or a floor of what is likely to happen:

1) The BJP's electoral dominance in terms of winning margins in the heartland states has significantly improved in 2019 compared to 1999, which puts the ruling party in good shape.

2) Even with their combined might as originally plotted, the alliance could muster only minor electoral gains based on the 2019 vote share distribution. The swing model suggests that in the event of a national wave towards the BJP, the ruling party is likely to make major gains in the states of West Bengal, Uttar Pradesh, Odisha and Telangana.

In the event of such a wave election, it is possible that its win rate will rival that of the Congress in the mid-1970s –

i.e. 75–80%. Given the uncertainty over the configuration of the Opposition and the very likely possibility of tail events happening, our forecast need not be considered fixed; indeed, it is not. It should be considered intelligent speculation, and just slightly more involved than who will bowl in the next over!

13

Conclusions – And Challenges Facing Modi and the Economy

The world is polarized, especially on ideology. In the US, there are heated arguments about Trump vs Biden. Over the last few decades (much less now), there was also divergence of opinion on monetarism vs fiscalism, on Keynes vs Friedman. There was much humour as well, from all sides. Robert Solow is reputed to have said, 'Another difference between Milton [Friedman] and myself is that everything reminds Milton of the money supply. Well, everything reminds me of sex, but I keep it out of my papers.'

Now, there is intelligent discussion and disagreement about the relationship, if any, between inflation and unemployment. But nowhere in the world, outside of India, do you see opinions, interpretations and cited facts being set at right angles to each other or 180 degrees apart (take your pick of the right metaphor!)

It is important to remind ourselves about the so-called Great Indian Poverty debate of the early 2000s. That debate was also civilized, a big fat book was written on it with contributions by participants (I plead guilty to being one of them) and we moved on. What was the debate about? The 1999–2000 CES had made the mistake of asking, 'How many tomatoes did you consume last *week?*' followed by, 'How many tomatoes did you consume last *month?*' Naturally, most individuals multiplied the 'week' estimate by four; some did not.

Nobel laureate Angus Deaton analysed the responses and concluded that the survey mis-design might have led to a lowering of the poverty estimate by 2% – close to a measurement error, given an overall poverty level of around 30%. Contrast that with the so-called poverty debate today. Real per capita consumption apparently increases by 40% and poverty also *increases* by a few percentage points! *'Yeh Kalyug hai ya kya hai?'* (Is this the age of darkness or what?).

In conclusion, I want to point out some counter-conclusions. Unreal poverty estimates have just been alluded to. In addition, UN employment projections show that the age group 15–64 will expand by a hundred million over the next decade, approximately by 10 million a year. Yet, 'International Domestic Scholars' (IDSs) maintain that more than 100 million jobs are needed over the next decade, with one prominent scholar (Ashoka Mody) estimating the need to be 200 million.

Official PLFS data show that the FLFPR is somewhere between 33% and 39%, depending on the employment definition. IDSs maintain, on the basis of CMIE data that they use instead of PLFS, that the Indian FLFPR is around

9%, the lowest in the world and well below Yemen. This passes as 'scholarly' work.

CMIE data on the number of jobs also vary substantially from PLFS data. After 2017–18 (when they broadly agree), CMIE says employment opportunities in the economy have dwindled, whereas PLFS claims that 64 million new jobs have been created in the last five years. Both cannot be right. So raise your hand if you think the CMIE data is anywhere close to reality. I see nothing. Case dismissed.

In an earlier chapter we talked about 'learning poverty', something the elite do not suffer from, which is why they are the elite. But if we ponder over the poor assessments of reality by elite scholars, domestic and international ... If we read what leading elite academics have said on a variety of subjects (growth, employment, labour force participation, consumption, poverty, investments, etc. – read this book!), then what does one conclude?

If we cannot agree on the facts, or rather if there are such huge discrepancies, then it is hard to have a debate. You can, for the purpose of argument, agree that 30% poverty is roughly the same as 32%, but an FLFPR of 33% cannot be reconciled with a rate of 9%.

And that's the question with which I want to conclude: do such debates happen elsewhere?

Do such debates with non-facts happen elsewhere? If not, why is India unique? A little soul-searching and narrative rejection is required of all.

For myself, 'I am mad as hell, and I am not going to take it any more!'[1]

Challenges for the future

India under Modi has been a unique experience – growth is good, and for once, whether in India or elsewhere, the political leadership has provided one of the most successful, Redistribution with Growth economies. After the election, Modi and India face the following challenges.

Delimitation and the north–south divide

There is no large country in the world where all regions develop at the same pace. It is a fact that in India, the south has developed at a faster pace than the north, and the south also pays a larger fraction of taxes. So? I fail to understand why there is a 'debate'. The only reason, perhaps, is that it is political.

The US constitution, in its infinite wisdom, almost 250 years ago had foreseen the potential *political* power problems that can arise if regions grow unequally in either population or wealth. They devised two power centres – a 'Lok Sabha' called the House of Representatives and a Senate with no equivalent in India.

We are a young democracy, and we have time on our side. But thinking has to proceed by looking forward. PM Modi rightly articulated a developed country ambition by

2047; we need a parallel date for a reformed democratic parliamentary system. One that does not penalize a region for growing faster than average – and as a consequence of that faster growth, have lower growth in population. There already is an active discussion on the need and desirability of simultaneous elections; perhaps, can a new mandate be added?

But what until then, since a new delimitation exercise is long overdue and important bills are contingent on this delimitation? In this regard, the IMF's actions on the increase of quotas ('equal' to the problem of a fair allocation of parliamentary seats for different states) are revealing and helpful: the advice would be to kick the can down the road. Parliament can be expanded, but in a proportionate manner with each state retaining the same fraction of seats in Parliament.

Reform of agriculture: the overdue farm laws

The proposal to reform agriculture, a long-neglected area of reform, was hijacked by insincere politics – is there any other kind? Again, lessons from other people's history are relevant. In 1994, the US, Mexico and Canada entered into a trade agreement (the North American Free Trade Agreement, or NAFTA). Before doing so, the negotiators had to solve the Mexican corn problem. Corn to Mexicans is like wheat to Punjab or rice to West Bengal. It is their staple, and culture, politics and economics are involved in its cultivation, production and marketing. There was one major problem – the Mexicans were most inefficient at producing corn (their production costs were much higher than costs prevailing in the US and Canada). What to do?

Give birth to cash transfers. DBT was not a household terms in any part of the world in 1994. But all economists and policymakers owe gratitude to this innovative and far-reaching concept. Actually, it is a very old concept – reform means one should buy out the losers. And that is what NAFTA agreement did. Mexican corn farmers were compensated for their profits from corn cultivation for a number of years during the period before NAFTA came into force. The farmers could grow anything but corn. Corn growing in Mexico was reformed, and we all lived happily ever after.[2]

Lessons and policies

Water is a problem in Punjab because of the profitability of rice cultivation. Buy out the problem. Pollution is a problem from crop burning – machines can do the job of threshing rice and planting wheat. As an economist might say – go for incentives, stupid.

Tax reform

Good policies beget better policies. Hence, the popularity and success of economic reforms. In a bold move, India reformed the corporate tax schedule in 2018. Direct tax reform is awaited. Just as in the case of corporate taxes, policymakers should recognize that tax reforms (read tax cuts) can lead to increased revenue through greater compliance and a more efficient economic system. Reform of direct taxes is long overdue and has been in the policy space for at least 15 years. It's time this particular bullet was bitten for the gain of all.

GST reform

GST taxation is a mega success story and one forecast by most economists. Now that it is part of our daily lives, it's time to bring incremental structural reform. Tax rates are too high and hurt the poor and the middle class. The average GST tax rate needs to be reduced. Time to bring progressivity to GST.

Data, statistics and progress: last item and possibly the most important

Galli galli mein shor hain ke hamare data mein problem hain. (In every street, there is a war cry – our statistical system, and its management, sucks)

This book is about data and its use. It is difficult to find any observer, international or domestic, who does not think that India needs to debureaucratize and depoliticize its data collection, reporting and dissemination. And no bans, please. If data is collected, it should be released. If there are mistakes made in collection or analysis, data collection is the easiest way to pinpoint those and to improve its quality. Everybody is better off. If data is not collected, everyone is worse off.

Surely, the senior administrators have more important things to worry about than the possible signals a particular piece of data will give to the voter. Better data will help in better-informed public policy, hence better service to all. And it is the easiest of reforms to undertake.

This book doesn't claim to be a comprehensive analysis of voter choices in 2024. I have looked at some of the hot-button issues that will undoubtedly influence choices, with a particular focus on economic issues. There will surely be other determinants of choice when we get down to granular levels of specific constituencies and of individual voters and candidates.

All countries have a problem with their statistics, and most make a constant effort at improvement. Private sector statistics act as checks and balances on government data. India has a particular problem with its survey collection and operations. There is no time schedule that is adhered to, and seemingly few controls on data quality. Given our expertise with software, this would seem to be an easy fix. Part of the problem is that the private sector, which should keep the checks and balances, is not cooperating; often, it offers even worse quality survey data. Public sector Delhi and private sector Mumbai – we have a data problem.

There is a Mexican stand-off – and all of us are losers. Hence, many people don't trust data per se and this is why it is possible for opponents of the government to float 'data-driven' narratives with assertions that are not only completely different from the official data but orthogonal to any reality.

What the official data tells us is that a large number of voters have reason to be satisfied with the performance of this government because their lives have gotten better between 2019 and 2024. Very few voters will feel the need to look at data when they make their choices – they know whether their lives have gotten better or worse.

According to psephological data and our simulations, the I.N.D.I.A. partnership would need a swing of well over 7% in vote share to overtake the BJP/NDA in 2024. I don't think that's likely.

It's the economy, stupid.

References

Anckar, Carsten and Fredriksson, Cecilia. (2018). 'Classifying Political Regimes 1800–2016: A Typology and a New Dataset.' *European Political Science.* doi:10.1057/s41304-018-0149-8.

Bernhard, M., Nordstrom, T. and Reenock, C. (2001). 'Economic Performance, Institutional Intermediation, and Democratic Survival', *Journal of Politics*, 63(3), 775–803. doi: 10.1111/0022-3816.00087.

Bhalla, Surjit S. (2019). 'The Most Off-Track of Them All', *Indian Express.* https://indianexpress.com/article/opinion/columns/gdp-economy-narendra-modi-arvind-subramanian-finance-5793864/.

Bhalla, S., Bhasin, K. and Virmani, M.A. (2022). 'Pandemic, Poverty, and Inequality: Evidence from India', International Monetary Fund.

Bhalla, S., and Das, Tirthatanmoy (2018). 'Population, Education, and Employment in India: 1983–2018', EAC website. https://eacpm.gov.in/wp-content/uploads/2018/12/population-education-and-employment-in-India-1983-2018.pdf.

Bhalla, S., Bhasin, K. and Das, Tirthatanmoy (2024). 'Female Labor Force Participation in India: Measurement in Times of Structural Change', report for the World Bank.

References

Bollen, K.A. and Paxton P. (2000). 'Subjective Measures of Liberal Democracy.' *Comparative Political Studies*, 33(1), 58–86. doi:10.1177/0010414000033001003.

Bollen, K.A. (2001). 'Cross-National Indicators of Liberal Democracy, 1950–1990'. https://doi.org/10.3886/ICPSR02532.v2.

Cattaneo, M., Jansson, M. and Ma, X. (2020). 'Simple Local Polynomial Density Estimators', EconPapers. https://econpapers.repec.org/paper/cdleconwp/qt9vt997qn.htm.

Chibber, P. and Verma, R. (2009). 'The Rise of the Second Dominant Party System in India: BJP's New Social Coalition in 2019', Studies in Indian Politics, Lokniti, Center for the Study of Developing Societies.

Coppedge, M, Alvarez A. and Maldonado C. (2008). 'Two Persistent Dimensions of Democracy: Contestation and Inclusiveness.' *Journal of Politics*, 70(03), 632–47. doi:10.1017/S0022381608080663.

Coppedge, M. and Reinicke W.H. (1990). 'Measuring Polyarchy.' *Studies in Comparative International Development*, 25(1), 51–72. doi:10.1007/Bf02716905.

Das, S. (2023). 'Democratic Backsliding in the World's Largest Democracy', SSRN. https://papers.ssrn.com/sol3/papers.cfm?abstract_id=4512936&download=yes.

Dreze, Jean and Somanchi, Anmol. (2023). 'Weighty Evidence? Estimating Poverty With Missing Data'. https://www.ideasforindia.in/topics/poverty-inequality/weighty-evidence-poverty-estimation-with-missing-data.html.

Financial Times (2024). 'A New Global Gender Divide Is Emerging'. https://www.ft.com/content/29fd9b5c-2f35-41bf-9d4c-994db4e12998.

References

Freedom House (2023). 'Freedom in the World 2023: Marking 50 Years in the Struggle for Democracy.' https://freedomhouse.org/report/freedom-world/2023/marking-50-years.

Kapoor, M. (2023). Political Claims and Statistical Findings: 'Fooled by Randomness'. https://www.muditkapoor.org/post/political-claims-and-statistical-findings-fooled-by-randomness.

Karnik, Ajit, Lalvani, Mala and Manali Phatak (2023). 'Political Incumbency Effects in India: A Regional Analysis', *Studies in Economics and Econometrics*, DOI: 10.1080/03796205.2023.2185666.

Kaufmann, D. and Kraay A. (2020). 'Worldwide Governance Indicators.' http://www.govindicators.org.

Gupta, S. (2023). '2024 Isn't about North vs South. See BJP's Limitations and Do the Maths, *The Print*. https://theprint.in/national-interest/2024-isnt-about-north-vs-south-see-bjps-limitations-do-the-maths/1878374/.

Little, Andrew and Meng, Anne (2023). 'Measuring Democratic Backsliding'. *PS: Political Science & Politics*. http://dx.doi.org/10.2139/ssrn.4327307.

Marquez, X. (2016). 'A Quick Method for Extending the Unified Democracy Scores'. https://papers.ssrn.com/sol3/papers.cfm?abstract_id=2753830 .

Márquez, X. (2020). 'democracyData: A Package for Accessing and Manipulating Existing Measures of Democracy.' http://github.com/xmarquez/democracyData.

Marshall, M.G. and Gurr, T.R. (2020). 'Polity 5: Political Regime Characteristics and Transitions, 1800–2018'. Dataset Users' Manual.

Marshall, M.G., Gurr, T.R and Jaggers, K. (2019). 'Polity IV Project:

Political Regime Characteristics and Transitions, 1800–2018'. Dataset Users' Manual.

McCrary et al. (2007). 'Manipulation of the Running Variable in the Regression Discontinuity Design: A Density Test,' *Journal of Econometrics*. https://www.sciencedirect.com/science/article/abs/pii/S0304407607001133.

Næss, A. (1956). *Democracy, Ideology, and Objectivity: Studies in the Semantics and Cognitive Analysis of Ideological Controversy*, Norwegian Research Council for Science and the Humanities.

Ozturk, O. (2021). 'Democratic Erosion in India: A Case Study, Democratic Erosion'. https://www.democratic-erosion.com/2021/02/05/democratic-erosion-in-india-a-case-study/.

Pemstein, D., Marquardt, K.L., Tzelgov, E., Wang, Y., Medzihorsky, J., Krusell, J., Miri, F., von Römer, J. (2022). 'The V-Dem Measurement Model: Latent Variable Analysis for Cross-National and Cross-Temporal Expert-Coded Data.' Technical Report 21, Varieties of Democracy Institute, University of Gothenburg. https://www.v-dem.net/media/filer_public/25/cb/25cb3f3f-290d-46e1-8eaf-ff2d2c13f4a9/v-dem_working_paper_21.pdf .

Pemstein, D., Meserve, S., Melton, J. (2010). 'Democratic Compromise: A Latent Variable Analysis of Ten Measures of Regime Type.' *Political Analysis*, 18(4), 426–49. doi:10.1093/pan/mpq020.

Pemstein, D., Meserve, S.A. and Melton, J. (2013). 'Replication Data for Democratic Compromise: A Latent Variable Analysis of Ten Measures of Regime Type'. http://hdl.handle.net/1902.1/PMM.

References

Rai, P. (2017). 'The Decline of the Congress Party in Indian Politics', *Economic and Political Weekly*. https://www.epw.in/journal/2017/12/web-exclusives/decline-congress-party-indian-politics.html.

Rutgers (2024). 'Gender Gap: Voting Choices in Presidential Elections (no date) Center for American Women and Politics.' https://cawp.rutgers.edu/gender-gap-voting-choices-presidential-elections.

Sanyal, S. and Arora, A. (2022). 'Why India Does Poorly on Global Perception Indices. https://eacpm.gov.in/wp-content/uploads/2022/11/Global-perception-indices_Final_22_Nov.pdf.

Saiarav (2023). The Ashoka paper-a case of democratic backsliding or academic backsliding?, Medium. Available at: https://medium.com/@yajnavalkya10/the-ashoka-paper-a-case-of-democratic-backsliding-or-academic-backsliding-37adf09b467a (Accessed: 29 January 2024).

Sklar, A. (2020). 'Democratic Erosion in India: The World's Largest Democracy No More?', Democratic Erosion. https://www.democratic-erosion.com/2020/02/12/democratic-erosion-in-india-the-worlds-largest-democracy-no-more/ (Accessed: 18 February 2024).

The Economist Intelligence Unit (2023). 'Democracy Index 2022: Frontline Democracy and the Battle for Ukraine.' https://www.eiu.com/n/wp-content/uploads/2023/02/Democracy-Index-2022_FV2.pdf?li_fat_id=f1fbad7e-a282-4b9e-9f8f-6a6d5a9fe6b8.

References

United Nations, Department of Economic and Social Affairs, Population Division (2022). 'World Population Prospects 2022: Methodology of the United Nations Population Estimates and Projections (UN DESA/POP/2022/TR/NO. 4)'.

Vogl, Tom S. et al. (2013). 'Race and the Politics of Close Elections', *Journal of Public Economics*. https://www.sciencedirect.com/science/article/abs/pii/S0047272713002144.

YouGov (2019). https://d25d2506sfb94s.cloudfront.net/cumulus_uploads/document/dg6dv6v8z0/Internal_PolAttention_191125.pdf.

Notes

2. What Determines Our Vote? Caste, Religion, Economy?

1   See Bhalla-Bhasin (2024) and Chapter 7 for a discussion on growth comparisons.

3. The Challenge of the Nehru Record

1   Nehru did not contest a fourth election; he passed away in 1964, two years into his third term.

4. The Democracy in Democracies

1   *Abhinav Motheram contributed to this chapter.*
2   S. Sanyal and A. Arora, 'Why India Does Poorly on Global Perception Indices', EAC-PM Working Paper Series, November 2022, https://eacpm.gov.in/wp-content/uploads/2022/11/Global-perception-indices_Final_22_Nov.pdf.
3   Andrew Little and Anne Meng, 'Measuring Democratic Backsliding', *PS: Political Science & Politics*, 18 July 2023, http://dx.doi.org/10.2139/ssrn.4327307.

5. Majority Rule and Minority Experience

1 *Abhinav Motheram contributed to this chapter.*
2 Kallol Bhattacherjee, 'Barack Obama Says India May "Pull Apart" Over Minority Rights', *The Hindu*, 23 June 2023, https://www.thehindu.com/news/national/barack-obama-says-india-may-pull-apart-over-minority-rights/article66998819.ece.
3 Selig Harrison, *India: The Most Dangerous Decades*, Princeton University Press, 1960.
4 Speech at the INC National Economic Conclave, 2022.
5 Valerie Wilson and William Darity, Jr., 'Understanding Black–White Disparities in Labor Market Outcomes Requires Models That Account for Persistent Discrimination and Unequal Bargaining Power', Economic Policy Institute, 25 March 2022, https://www.epi.org/unequalpower/publications/understanding-black-white-disparities-in-labor-market-outcomes/.
6 Shahid Javed Burki, 'The Story of the Other India', *The Express Tribune*, 25 December 2023, https://tribune.com.pk/story/2451061/the-story-of-the-other-india.

6. Democratic Backsliding in India – Some Narrative 'Evidence'

1 *Abhinav Motheram contributed to this chapter.*
2 Andrew Little and Anne Meng, 'Measuring Democratic Backsliding', *PS: Political Science & Politics*, 18 July 2023, p. 28, http://dx.doi.org/10.2139/ssrn.4327307.
3 Sabyasachi Das, 'Democratic Backsliding in the World's Largest Democracy', The Social Science Research Network, 25 July 2023, http://dx.doi.org/10.2139/ssrn.4512936.

4   M. Kapoor, 'Political Claims and Statistical Findings: "Fooled by Randomness"', 22 August 2023, https://www.muditkapoor. org/post/political-claims-and-statistical-findings-fooled-by-randomness.

5   Tom S. Vogl et al., 'Race and the Politics of Close Elections', *Journal of Public Economics*, January 2014, https://www. sciencedirect.com/science/article/abs/pii/S0047272713002144.

6   Yajnavalkya, 'The Ashoka Paper – A Case of Democratic Backsliding or Academic Backsliding?', Medium, 10 August 2023, https://medium.com/@yajnavalkya10/the-ashoka-paper-a-case-of-democratic-backsliding-or-academic-backsliding-37adf09b467a.

7. Giving Birth to Economic Narratives

1   Table 2.1 in Chapter 2 provided empirical evidence about the irrelevance of inflation for election outcomes – especially in contrast to growth.

2   Surjit Bhalla, Karan Bhasin and Arvind Virmani, 'Pandemic, Poverty, and Inequality: Evidence from India', *IMF Working Papers*, 5 April 2022, https://www.imf.org/en/Publications/WP/Issues/2022/04/05/Pandemic-Poverty-and-Inequality-Evidence-from-India-516155.

8. Mother of All Narratives – Jobs and Unemployment and Wages

1   There are several experts, and I don't want to offend someone because I did not mention them. Strictly in alphabetical order:

Ashoka Mody, Himanshu, Maitreesh Ghatak, Pronab Sen, Raghuram Rajan.

2 Surjit S. Bhalla and Tirthatanmoy Das, 'Population, Education, and Employment in India: 1983–2018', EAC-PM website, https://eacpm.gov.in/wp-content/uploads/2018/12/population-education-and-employment-in-India-1983-2018.pdf.

3 'Why Prof. Ashoka Mody Believes India Is Broken', Princeton International, 1 March 2023, https://international.princeton.edu/news/why-prof-ashoka-mody-believes-india-broken.

4 https://population.un.org/wpp/.

5 https://ilostat.ilo.org/data/.

6 This is obtained from the Labour Bureau surveys, Bhalla-Das 2018, p. 19.

7 Jean Drèze and Anmol Somanchi, 'Weighty Evidence? Poverty Estimation with Missing Data', Ideas for India (I4I), 10 April 2023, https://www.ideasforindia.in/topics/poverty-inequality/weighty-evidence-poverty-estimation-with-missing-data.html.

8 John Reed and Andy Lim, 'In Charts: How India Has Changed Under Narendra Modi', *Financial Times*, 9 January 2024, https://www.ft.com/content/8299d318-7c35-49a0-9a9a-b8e5abeba7be.

9 https://alpinemacro.com/blog/.

9. Gender Advances to the Top in India and the World

1 'Full text of PM Narendra Modi's 70th Independence Day Speech', *The Economic Times*, 15 August 2016, https://

economictimes.indiatimes.com/news/politics-and-nation/full-text-of-pm-narendra-modis-70th-independence-day-speech/articleshow/53710263.cms?from=mdr.

2 S. Bhalla, K. Bhasin and Tirthatanmoy Das, 'Female Labor Force Participation in India: Measurement in Times of Structural Change', March 2024, report for the World Bank.

3 John Reed and Andy Lim, 'In Charts: How India Has Changed Under Narendra Modi', *Financial Times*, 9 January 2024, https://www.ft.com/content/8299d318-7c35-49a0-9a9a-b8e5abeba7be.

10. Elimination of Extreme Poverty in India – Will It Affect Choice 2024?

1 Maitreesh Ghatak and Rishabh Kumar, 'The Simmering Debate Over Poverty Rate', *Mint*, 4 May 2023, https://www.livemint.com/economy/the-simmering-debate-over-poverty-rate-11683142431495.html.

2 https://dbtbharat.gov.in/.

3 www.worldbank.pip.

11. Redistribution with Growth

1 Elif C. Arbatli Saxegaard et al., 'Inequality and Poverty in India: Impact of Covid-19 Pandemic and Policy Response', *IMF Working Papers*, 14 July 2023, https://www.imf.org/en/Publications/WP/Issues/2023/07/20/Inequality-and-Poverty-in-India-Impact-of-Covid-19-Pandemic-and-Policy-Response-535908.

2 Surjit S. Bhalla and Karan Bhasin, 'Whose Economic Performance Was Better, UPA or NDA? Growth Rates Don't Tell the Whole Story', The Print, 19 January 2023, https://theprint.in/opinion/whose-economic-performance-was-better-upa-or-nda-growth-rates-dont-tell-the-whole-story/1928162/.

3 Surjit S. Bhalla and Karan Bhasin, 'India—China: Reversal of Fortunes?', The Brookings Institution, 14 September 2023, https://www.brookings.edu/articles/india-china-reversal-of-fortunes/.

12. Not Forecast 2024, But . . .

1 *Abhinav Motheram contributed to this chapter.*

2 'Shri L.K. Advaniji's Blog "It Is Not Faith Versus Law, It Is Faith Upheld By Law"', bjp.org, 3 October 2010, https://www.bjp.org/pressreleases/shri-lk-advanijis-latest-blog-it-not-faith-versus-law-it-faith-upheld-law.

3 Saaket Jain, 'Narendra Modi the Citizen Can Attend Ayodhya "Bhoomi Pujan", But Prime Minister Shouldn't', The Wire, 4 August 2020, https://thewire.in/government/prime-minister-narendra-modi-ayodhya-bhoomi-pujan.

4 'Shri L.K. Advaniji's latest blog "It Is Not Faith Versus Law, It Is Faith Upheld by Law"', Bharatiya Janata Party, 3 October 2010, https://www.bjp.org/pressreleases/shri-lk-advanijis-latest-blog-it-not-faith-versus-law-it-faith-upheld-law.

5 Shekhar Gupta, '2024 Isn't About North vs South. See BJP's Limitations & Do the Maths', The Print, 9 December 2023, https://theprint.in/national-interest/2024-isnt-about-north-vs-south-see-bjps-limitations-do-the-maths/1878374/.

13. Conclusions – And Challenges Facing Modi and the Economy

1 One of the most telling speeches about frustration at the mad world – from the film *Network*, 1976.

2 Santiago Levy, 'Progress against Poverty: Sustaining Mexico's Progresa Oportunidades Program', Brookings Institution Press, 2006, https://www.brookings.edu/books/progress-against-poverty/.

Acknowledgements

We would like to thank Karan Bhasin, Kirti Dave, Ravinder Kaur and Pranjal Mishra for helpful comments and discussion.